Legalistic Way

Lessons From XunZi and Han Fei Zi

DR SHEH SEOW WAH

First Published 2011

Published by Dr Sheh Seow Wah
ISBN: 13 9781 4636 12993
ISBN: 10 1463612990

Edited by Sharon Chelvi
Ganesamoorthy

Published in Singapore

Printed in Malaysia

CONTENTS

Acknowledgements

This book is dedicated to those who are interested to know more about the Chinese mind especially the Legalistic School and how they relate to contemporary business, leadership and organizational practices.

I would like to dedicate this book to my mum, Poon King Hiang, my sisters, Sheh Siew Cheng and Sheh Siew Chen, my brother, Cheng Wei Hao. I would also like to express my deepest gratitude to my late father, Sheh Kak Fa.

Other Books:

- ***"Chinese Management" – 138 pages (1995)***
- ***"Chinese Wisdom on Life and Management" – 148 pages (1998 – in English) and (1999- in Indonesian)***
- ***"Chinese Leadership: Moving from Classical to Contemporary" – 174 pages (2003) and e-book version (2009)***
- ***"The Natural Way: Lessons From Lao Zi and Zhuang Zi" – 219 pages (2009)***
- ***"The Humanistic Way: Lessons From Confucius and Mencius" – 202 pages (2010)***
- ***"The Strategic Way: Lessons From the Chinese Strategic Thinker" – 269 pages (2010)***

佘绍华博士

A Review of the Classical Chinese Legalistic School

Over the past 4,000-5,000 years of civilization, China has been ruled by few hundreds of kings or emperors. In China, knowledge of philosophy is more important than religion (Moore, 1967). Philosophy plays a very significant role in the life of the average Chinese, even that of the common man. This is particularly true for the intellectual or the educated man. This section will review three key philosophical developments in China, namely the humanistic school, the legalistic school and the naturalistic school. The review will take a more descriptive approach rather than a critical and evaluative one. Each school of thought has its own merits and demerits and has its usefulness and appropriateness in resolving problems in different times and situations. As such, it is not useful to attach a value judgment to any specific approach, while returning to the notion that each approach is equally good as it is appropriate to its historical context.

Through a systematic study of the Chinese classics and history, it is not difficult to uncover the rich body of works about social and political philosophies, as well as the philosophy of life. These philosophies evolved from the school of humanism espoused by Confucius and Mencius, to utilitarianism by Mozi and legalism by Xunzi and Han Fei Zi, and finally to the naturalism of Lao Zi and Zhuang Zi. To examine the relevance and implications of Confucius, Mencius, Han Fei Zi, Xunzi, Lao Zi and Zhuang Zi's works in the present day context requires re-interpretation and re-organization. Re-interpretation will provide new meanings to these ancient teachings so as to keep it on par with man's civilization and modernization. Still, while it is essential to continuously seek improvements in our organizational practices, it is of paramount importance to retain at least a shadow of the ancient wisdom.

What is the underlying assumption about human nature? Are people by nature good or bad? People have debated about human nature for thousands of years; some religions or philosophers assume that a person is born evil, while others believe a person is born good. If a person's innate nature is good it will include kindness, humility, generosity and helpfulness, while if a person's innate nature is evil it will include jealousy, selfishness, violence, deceit and wickedness.

Confucius and Mencius believed that man's nature is naturally good. Based on the assumption that human nature is good, one would be able to cultivate a person's character and train one's personality through education and earnest practice (a developmental orientation). If a ruler was virtuous and benevolent, he would set the right example for the people to follow and thus, the people would become good citizens. This metaphor is in line with Theory Y as advocated by Douglas McGregor in the 1950's – man likes to work and treats working as a natural process.

Mencius was born a century or so after the death of Confucius (Lau, 1970). To Mencius, defining human nature as neither good nor bad is as good as saying human beings have an equal tendency of being either good or bad from birth. Although the natural characteristics of water do not show any preference for either following east or west (right or left), it definitely has a preference for flowing downwards instead of upwards. He endorsed the philosophy that human beings are by nature good, just as water naturally has the tendency to flow downwards. Mencius said, *"There is no man who is no good; there is not water that does not flow downwards."* (Book VI: A:1 of Mencius – Lau, 1970).

On the other hand, Xunzi (also known as "Hsun-tze") and Han Fei Zi advocated that man's nature is naturally evil. Thus, strict rules and severe punishments were used to circumscribe human behavior (a control orientation). Both Xunzi and Han Fei Zi felt that it is naïve to think that human nature is good. To them, men are born bad, with a natural self-interest. This metaphor is in line with Theory X as espoused by Douglas McGregor – man is lazy and dislikes work and if possible, will try to avoid it. In Book 23.1 of Xunzi's works, he wrote, *"Human nature is evil; any good in humans is acquired by conscious exertion."*

an from Abba. She is opposed to the relationship
ιot officially married (no bride price paid yet) plus

nigbo's mother. To break up Olanna and Odenigbo
ts pregnant but after giving birth, she refuses to take

parents. Chief Okonji claims a romantic interest in

s and father to Olanna and Kainene. Chief Ozobia
also keeps a mistress, and eventually leaves Nigeria

; wife and mother of Olanna and Kainene. She does
ıd her marriage with Chief Ozobi might be described

)f Olanna's mother. He lives with his family in Kano

ves guidance to Olanna, who isn't very close to her

.unty Ifeka's daughter. Arize is eager find a husband
anna.

(Knoblock, 1999). In Book 23.4, 23.5 and 23.9, Xunzi directly confronted Mencius's assumption that human nature is good. In Book 23.4, Xunzi said, *"Mencius contended that 'since man can learn, his nature is good.' I say that this is not so. It shows that Mencius did not reach any real understanding of what man's inborn nature is and that he did not investigate the division between those things that are inborn in man and those that are acquired……"* (Knoblock, 1999). In the above paragraph, Xunzi discussed the concepts of 'nature' versus 'nurture' in distinguishing man's behavior. What Mencius referred to as human nature, Xunzi counted as nurture. Even in today's study of psychology, the debate between what behaviors can be constituted as 'natural' and 'nurtured' cannot reach a conclusive answer.

In Book 23.4, Xunzi further described,

"…… As a general rule, 'inborn nature' embraces what is spontaneous from Nature, what cannot be learned, and what requires no application to master. Ritual principles and moral duty are creations of the sages. They are things that people must study to be able to follow them and to which they must apply themselves before they can fulfil their precepts. What cannot be gained by learning and cannot be mastered by application yet is found in man is properly termed 'inborn nature'. What must be learned before a man can do it and what he must apply himself to before he can master it yet is found in man is properly called 'acquired nature'. This is precisely the distinction between 'inborn' and 'acquired' natures……" (Knoblock, 1999).

The argument between what is natural and what is nurtured is that whatever is natural does not need to be learned. For example, a baby crying when he or she is hungry is not showing learned behavior but rather its inborn nature. Many of our human desires are inborn but we have learned to 'curb' them throughout the development of mankind. In Book 23.5, Xunzi further argued against Mencius's viewpoint that man is born naturally good by describing how man's evil behaviors are acquired rather than inborn. Xunzi said,

"Mencius said: Now, the nature of man is good, so the cause (of evil) is that all men lose or destroy their original nature. I say that

portraying man's inborn nature like this transgresses the truth. Now, it is man's nature that as soon as he is born, he begins to depart from his original simplicity and his childhood naiveté so that of necessity they are lost or destroyed. (If we consider the implications of these facts, it is plain that man's nature is evil). Those who say man's inborn nature is good admire what does not depart from his original simplicity and think beneficial what is not separated from his childhood naiveté. They treat these admirable qualities and the good that is in man's heart and thoughts as though they were inseparably linked to his inborn nature, just as seeing clearly is to the eye and hearing acutely is to the ear. Thus, inborn nature they say is 'like the clear sight of the eye and the acute hearing of the ear.'" (Knoblock, 1999).

To Mencius, man is born kind and good and it is through interaction and socialization that one's good nature will be lost. Should nature or culture come first? Lao Zi and Zhuang Zi often refer to Nature and its characteristics as the guiding principles for humans. We learn our culture from our ancestors. Where do our ancestors learn their culture from? It must be first from Nature; Nature is our first teacher. Both argued that civilization, when social norms and values were established, gave rise to hypocritical and deceitful people. The true nature of the people was lost. Through civilization and cultural influence, human beings have lost their original nature. This idea is against Confucius's and Mencius's argument that man should be cultivated through moral rituals and learning. To Confucius, virtue pervades all aspects of one's life. Once a person acquires the right virtues, he or she will lead a decent life and be a good citizen. A person should learn to acquire all these virtues from young before acquiring other knowledge. Education should start from young and at home. It is these Confucian values that make an individual noble, and thus evolves an orderly and harmonious society and a peaceful world.

Both have interesting views about what is man's nature. For example, the original nature of bamboo is its ability to float if tossed into a river. However, if one splits a bamboo piece into strips, bundles them together and tosses them into the river again, the bundle of strips will sink. The original nature of the bamboo is lost after the splitting. So, which part of man's behavior is the original nature of man and which is nurture? This is debatable. Xunzi further argued about man's nature being evil in his Book 23.9, where he said,

"Mencius claims that man's nature is good. I say that this is not so. As a rule, from antiquity to the present day, what the world has called good is what is correct, in accord with natural principles, peaceful, and well-ordered. What has been called evil is what is wrong through partiality, what wickedly contravenes natural principles, what is perverse, and what is rebellious. This is precisely the division between the good and the evil. Now, can one truly take man's inborn nature to have as its essential characteristics correctness, accord with natural principles, peacefulness, and order? Were that the case, what use would there be for sage kings, and what need for ritual and moral principles! And even supposing that there were sage kings and rituals and moral principles, what indeed could they add to correctness, natural principles, peace, and order!

Now, of course this is not so. The nature of man is evil. Thus, in antiquity the sages considered his nature evil, to be inclined to prejudice and wickedness, and not toward uprightness, to be perverse and rebellious, and not be orderly. Thus, they established the authority of lords and superiors to supervise men, elucidated ritual and moral principles to transform both, set up laws and standards to bring them to order, and piled on penal laws and punishments to restrain them. They caused the entire world to develop with good order and to be consistent with the good. Such was the government of the sage Kings and the transforming influence of ritual and moral principles.

Now, let us try to imagine a situation where we do away with the authority of lords and superiors, do without the transforming influence of ritual and morality, discard the order provided by the laws and rectitude, do without the restraints of penal laws and punishments – were this to occur, let us consider how the people of the world would deal with each other. In such a situation the strong would inflict harm on the weak and rob them; the many would tyrannize the few and wrest their possessions from them; and the perversity and rebelliousness of the whole world would quickly ensure their mutual destruction. If we consider the implications of these facts, it is plain that human nature is evil and that any good in humans is acquired by conscious exertion." (Knoblock, 1999)

Here, Xunzi subscribed to the assumption that man's nature is evil but can be corrected through moral rituals and learning. Unlike him, Han Fei Zi, the student of Xunzi, believed that man's nature cannot be corrected and as such it needs to be circumscribed by laws and rules. In Book 23.10, Xunzi challenged Mencius's assumption that man's nature is good by saying that Mencius's assumption and thesis lacked evidence and consistency. He then argued that if man's nature is good, then one could dispense with having a wise ruler and a set of ritual and moral principles. It is because man's nature is evil, that the importance of having a wise ruler (or Sage) accompanied by a set of ritual and moral principles to circumscribe human behavior became an essential.

Based on the works of Confucius and Mencius as well as Mozi, Xunzi and Han Fei Zi, the following dimension as per Figure 1 was developed.

Figure 1: Different Dimensions of Chinese Philosophies

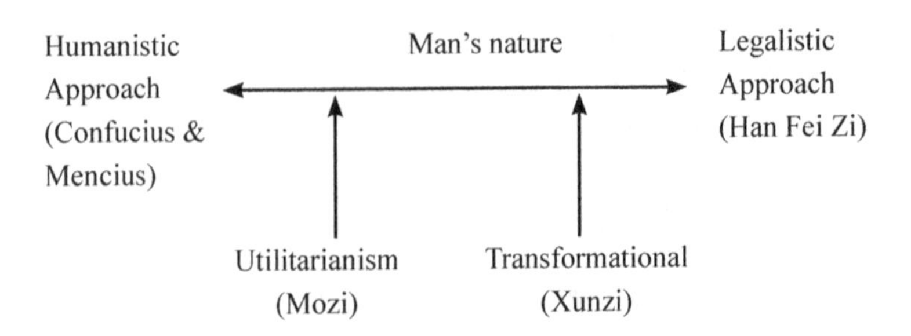

As discussed earlier, both Confucius and Mencius believed that human beings were fundamentally good. Mozi a utilitarian believed that humans should engage in activities that directly benefit others, particularly in agriculture. He did not debate much about human nature but rather focused on their behaviors and how they should act in order to benefit themselves and others. During the warring states era, Chinese politics became more corrupt and cynical. Many philosophers from the schools of Confucianism and Mozi called for ethical reform. As for the Daoists, they preferred to let nature take its course or retreated into seclusion. The Daoists subscribed to 'wu-wei' – that means doing nothing or non-interference. The emphasis on moral and ethical behavior of the individual and governments was strongly supported by the School of Legalism. To make people moral, the legalists put forward the notion of 'rule by law' where the law should be placed above the individual and the individual rulers as well. Nobody is above the law.

Mozi, whose original name was Mo Di (470-391 BC) was the founder of Mohism. Mozi was one of the Chinese philosophers during the hundred schools of thought period within the early Warring States Era. He was a carpenter by profession and did not hold any official position. Mozi was a follower of Confucianism but he felt that Confucianism was too fatalistic and emphasized too much on elaborate celebrations and funerals which were counter-productive to the common people. One of the core theses of Mohism is related to the virtue of frugality – that is frugality in expenditure and in funerals, and not to waste money on elaborate musical displays. Mozi was particularly against the Confucians for spending excessively on funeral rituals and musical displays that did not directly contribute to the welfare of the people.

Mozi's moral teachings emphasized self-reflection and authenticity rather than obedience to ritual. By reflecting on one's own successes and failures, one attains true self-knowledge rather than mere conformity to ritual. Mozi exhorted people to lead a life of asceticism and self-restraint, renouncing both material and spiritual extravagance

(Wales, Jimmy from Wikipedia in 2011). Mozi tended to evaluate actions based on whether they provided benefit to the people, which he measured in terms of an enlarged population, a prosperous economy, and social order. In many ways, Mozi's philosophy and thought is parallel to the Western utilitarian principle, where a person's actions should be measured by the way they contribute or bring benefits to the society at large. He paid attention to the day-to-day living of the commoners. In general, Mozi subscribed to the following, just to mention a few:

- Attract and promote capable people into the government by delegating the relevant power and responsibility to them and rewarding them appropriately. Recruitment should be based on meritocracy and not blood relations. A wise ruler should continuously treasure talented people and seek their counsel frequently. Although talented people are difficult to manage, they can contribute significantly to the welfare and wellbeing of a nation.

- Put the interest of others equal to the interest of self or else the world will be in trouble. In this respect, Mohism is best known for the concept of "Universal Love" – a person should care for all men equally regardless of their relationship to him or her.

- A good ruler or government should be frugal in expenditure. Moral values must be emphasized and cannot be compromised. To the Mohist, the ruler should exercise a high level of righteousness or else it would bring disaster to the nation. Without a benevolent ruler, trusted people will not be loyal and loyal people will not be trusted.

- To rule by standards rather than by emotion, is another important aspect of Mohism's political philosophy. A wise ruler should use law and order to circumscribe the people's behavior. A wise ruler would be better off depending on his "standard tools" to manage or rule his country rather than using his emotions.

- Mohists subscribe to the forming of political structure and hierarchy in order to implement any political ideas and translate them into a reality. Mohism strongly opposes any form of aggression, such as war with its neighbors or other states. To Mohists, peace is of utmost importance.

In Chapter 2 and 9 (de Bary, 1960), Mozi discussed the importance of having an effective structure with reporting relationships supported by the system of reward and punishment. To Mozi, in ancient times when structure and reporting relationships were not well-established, the country was in disorder. In order to restore social order, the most worthy and wise should emerge to lead the empire. As the capability of one person is limited, the empire has to be divided into 3 states with each state managed by a minister. The running of each state would then be supported by officials. Once the hierarchy has been established, the roles and responsibilities for each position are defined. In respect of reporting relationships, the lower level reports to the middle level and the middle level to the top level. The basis of the reward and punishment system is that the worthy will be exalted and promoted while the unworthy will be rejected and banished. In this manner, everybody will be encouraged by reward and deterred by punishment.

Being a utilitarian, Mozi emphasized the standardization of the law as well as its uniform enforcement. The legalists adopted Mozi's idea of standardization of law. In meting out the punishment, everybody is considered equal. Both Xunzi and Han Fei Zi subscribed to the notion that 'human nature is evil', but to Xunzi, man can be changed or reformed through acculturation and education. In contrast, Han Fei Zi believed that human nature can only be circumscribed through strict law and enforcement. To some extent, Han Fei Zi is a pure legalist. After the downfall of the Qin dynasty, Chinese rulers or governments practiced a concoction of humanism and legalism in governing the country for over 2,000 years.

By contrast, the school of Daoism espoused by Lao Zi is more metaphysical and abstract. The study of Dao entails how things happen and how things work. Lao Zi strongly endorsed allowing things to unfold by themselves. Lao Zi believed in being natural and subscribed to "wu-wei" which means "doing nothing or non-interference". As Dao is the principle of all things, Dao does not struggle but lets things unfold by themselves. Still, "wu-wei" does not suggest complete inactivity but to follow the natural laws and order. It is a natural way of behaving, which allows things to unfold based on their natural order. To Lao Zi and Zhuang Zi, the possible is possible; the impossible is impossible. Lao Zi's classics can be equated with Natural Law. As natural law embraces all events, both human and non-human, all natural principles are considered good and moral. The Natural Laws that describe and explain the Universe are also applicable to man.

Besides this, Lao Zi believed that all behavior consists of opposites or polarities, and thus, one must avoid extremes. All things and behavior embrace 'Yin' (passive or feminine property) and 'Yang' (active or masculine property). The understanding of 'Yin' and 'Yang' principles teaches one to avoid the extremes and move toward the 'middle path' or the practice of moderation. To Lao Zi, the concept of opposites exists only in our mind. When we recognize that something is good, the opposite (evil) becomes defined as well. The way we perceive our surroundings will naturally give rise to the opposite. Where there is impossibility, there is possibility. Where there is possibility, there is impossibility. There are two sides to a coin but we are talking about the same coin. Opposites co-exist in unity. In the exploration of Nature, many initial theories and concepts seem to oppose each other but in reality they complement each other. By learning to value the opposite, one is able to keep everything in a balanced position.

Thus, in the eyes of the Daoist, there is nothing absolutely good or evil. There is always evil within the good and good within the evil. Good cannot exist without evil or the absence of good is evil. Everything is defined by its opposite. If you say something is 'good', then the absence of it is 'evil'. The understanding of good and evil allows one to be more agile and alert when interacting with others. If you start to perceive others as good by nature, then you may reduce your guard against them. You will be opened up to others harming you. When meeting an acquaintance, it is important not to overly 'trust' a person until you know him or her better. On the other hand, if you start to perceive others as evil by nature then you may only 'see' the negative side of others and thus ignore their good points. In the Chinese culture, the middle path is to be adopted. There is a Chinese saying,

"One should not harbor an evil mind to harm others but must guard others from harming oneself."

In reviewing the different dimensions put forward by Confucius and Mencius (Humanism), Mozi (Utilitarianism), Xunzi and Han Fei Zi (Legalism) and Lao Zi and Zhuang Zi (Naturalism), each represents a different philosophy of life of the Chinese. In ancient times, the Chinese had high regard for the study of the philosophy of life, even more than science and technology. There has been much debate on the value of the study of philosophy against the study of science and technology. That has also becomes one of the key elements in differentiating between Chinese and Western culture. To the Chinese, philosophy is the knowledge amongst knowledge while a philosopher is a man amongst men (Moore, 1967). So, what is the ultimate purpose of life in the mind of the average Chinese? Based on the above four schools of thoughts, I have put forward the following:

Humanism (Confucius and Mencius)

The fundamental principle of Confucius's and Mencius's teaching is 'to love others' and the importance of self-cultivation, especially one's integrity and morality.

- To be able to love oneself is basic; before we learn to love others, we must first be able to love ourselves. To love oneself is different from pampering oneself;

- Next is the ability to love others, which includes our parents, siblings, relatives, neighbors, classmates, friends and colleagues. To love others is to protect them. This will ultimately evolve into an orderly and stable society;
- Then comes the ability to love the environment, and be environmentally-friendly; and
- Finally, preserving the environment for the future is to demonstrate the ability to love future generations ("The Spirit of Humanism").

Utilitarianism (Mozi or Mohism)

This is to create wealth to satisfy one's desires (physiological and psychological), which is the basic purpose of an individual's existence. Its key principles are:

- To devote efforts to create wealth, bring happiness and enjoy life. These are the basic elements of life. Be pragmatic by doing things that can really benefit others. Do not recommend things that cannot be put into practice;
- To share the fruits of one's efforts with your family members and thus extend your happiness to others – in order to promote "Universal Love";
- To contribute to the economic growth and development of society and thus, society can enjoy a higher level of prosperity. Life is not fair, especially in terms of the distribution of wealth among the rich and the poor. Thus, doing charity work or philanthropy s the best way to make society slightly less unfair ; and
- To carry forward the prosperity to future generations and continue to perpetuate wealth to infinity.

Legalism (Xunzi and Han Fei Zi)

The importance of religions, ritual and moral principles, laws, regulations and penal codes, and political systems have been emphasized in preserving an orderly and harmonious society.

- All religions encourage one to do good and avoid doing evil and thus they are useful ways to circumscribe evil thoughts and behaviors;
- Ritual and moral principles encourage one to refine oneself through learning. They preach a sense of righteousness (knowing what is right and what is wrong), a sense of justice, righteousness, trustworthiness and humaneness to circumscribe one's behaviors (a soft approach);
- Laws, regulations and penal codes serve as a deterrent to doing evil or even punish the one that violates or threatens social order (a hard approach); and
- Implementation of an appropriate political system that promotes personal freedom circumscribed by rule of law to ensure social order.

Naturalism (Lao Zi and Zhuang Zi)

Naturalism subscribes to "The Way" in explaining the Universe, and embraces the whole of creation and the creator. The natural principle sees no difference between the past and the present.

- Use one's experience to serve as the source of self-cultivation and self-preservation;
- Human existence, from the individual's birth to death, is transitory. Everything evolves like a cycle: life and death is no different from the four seasons;
- The individual is part of a family; a family is part of society; a society is part of a larger entity; and so on till it becomes the Universe, the Cosmos and Infinity. Thus, in evaluating the past, first study the present. In studying the multitudes, we must first study the few.
- The principle and system that explains the Universe (the larger system) is also applicable to the individual (a human being is the sub-system of a larger system); and
- All events (human and Natural) evolve based on the principle of Nature ("The Way") – which does not change.

CLASSICAL CHINESE PHILOSOPHICAL FRAMEWORK

Based on the brief review of the three different schools of the Chinese classics above, namely, humanism, legalism and naturalism which evolved during the Warring States and Spring and Autumn periods, a simple framework was developed as in Figure2.

Figure 2
Classical Chinese Philosophical Framework

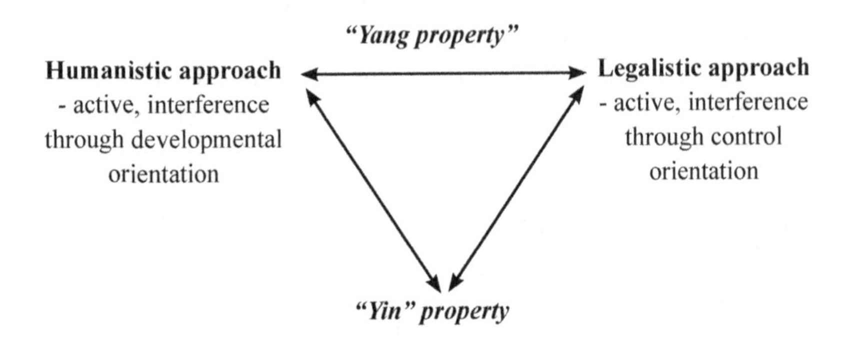

Naturalistic approach

- Passive, non-interference ('wu-wei'), receptive and yielding
- paradoxical integration

As described in Figure 2, Chinese philosophies can be briefly categorized into three schools of thoughts, that are the Confucian tradition, the Legalist tradition and the Daoist tradition. These three different schools have a different emphasis on the role of 'penal law' in maintaining social order. In the Confucian tradition, if a ruler regulates his people by laws, there will be no sense of shame. Confucian scholars did not dispute the necessity of penal laws in punishing those who committed crimes. The emphasis is that the ruler should first educate the people on morality and the importance of righteousness before meting out punishment. In the Legalist tradition, social order can only be maintained by penal law while ritual and moral principles only serve as reinforcement. The average legalist believed that the ruler should first deter any form of immoral activity before he can make the people moral. In the Daoist tradition, the concept of "wu wei" (non-action) takes precedence over interference. Thus, any form of interference, either the use of moral teachings or penal laws is unnecessary. Some of the key differences in emphasis on 'penal law' are summarized in Table 1.

Table 1: Key Differences in Interpretation of Penal Law

Confucian Tradition	Legalist Tradition
• Good laws by themselves are not sufficient in maintaining social order in the long run.	• Good laws are a necessary condition for proper social order.
• Laws and the consequent punishments should only be applied after efforts have been made to provide the people with the right moral education.	• Laws and harsh punishments should be the primary force to deter the people from doing immoral things. "Prevention is better than cure." Thereafter, efforts will be taken to make them moral.
• Moral education should be emphasized from a young age. Laws and punishment should only be applied to the few who have deviated.	• Efforts should be made to promulgate laws clearly and to ensure that people are fully aware and understand their contents and implications.
• A ruler should be bound by his own moral awareness first before being bound by the law.	• A ruler should be bound by his own law. He should use the law to regulate others to serve his own interests.
• In an ideal society, people should be regulated by moral values and then circumscribed by penal laws.	• In an ideal society, people should be regulated by penal laws with harsh punishments so that the people are afraid to do immoral things.

Source: "The Art of Rulership" by Roger T. Ames (1983)

THE SCHOOL OF LEGALISM

In Chinese writing, the word "法" can be interpreted in two ways:

- "standard or method"; or
- "penal law" or "rule of law".

Early Chinese scholars debated much about the importance of using "法" ("fa") in governing the state and in the maintenance of social order. Between 700 BC and 200 BC, China experienced a warring state with plenty of chaos – such as destruction, devastation, broken families, production destroyed and lives sacrificed. It was during uncertain or troubled times that China produced a great pool of philosophers, thinkers and strategists who tried to advise the various emperors and dynasties on how best to run an orderly, harmonious and strong nation. In order to make a nation strong, a ruler needs to:

- Unite the mind and behavior of the people;
- Circumscribe them with penal law;
- Encourage them with an effective reward system; and
- Lead them to a higher level of prosperity.

As the Chinese saying goes, "Chaos gives birth to the need for control." Control gives birth to the need for a system. This is what we call the **'System of Control' or 'Rule of Law'.**

In the middle of the sixth century BC, the 'Penal Code of Law' or penal law had become public knowledge and formed the system of political control in China (Ames, 1983). The emergence of the Legalist school that put emphasis on the notion of 'penal law' instead of 'moral conduct or influence', had been the property and responsibility of the ruling classes. The Legalist believed that it was more important to keep the people from doing 'evil' through strict laws than to encourage people to do 'good' through moral persuasion. The leader or ruler does not busy himself with morals but with laws (De bary, 1960 and Fung, 1948). Thus, government by law instead of government through individual leadership was emphasized (De bary, 1960). The origin of the School of Legalism was unclear. It is said that as far back as the 7th century BC it was put forward by the prime minister of Chi, Kuan Chung (around 645 BC). There are others who associated the School of Legalism to the 'Book of Lord Shang' authored by Shang Yang (around 338 BC). Later, it was Han Fei Zi (233-280 BC), the student of Xunzi, who based his political philosophy on the assumption that 'man by nature is evil' and thus needs to be controlled by strong government and strict laws.

Han Fei Zi's philosophical thought and principles were put into practice by the first emperor of China, Qin Shi Huang, who unified China in 221 BC. During the reign of Emperor Qin, many Confucian scholars were killed and Confucian texts were destroyed. During the Qin Dynasty, Emperor Qin Shi Huang together with his prime minister, Li Si (who was also a student of Xunzi), jointly enforced Legalist thought. However, the legalistic system only lasted for 14 years. In 207 BC, the Qin Dynasty was overthrown and replaced by the Han Dynasty. From the Han Dynasty up till the present day, the Chinese government has mainly subscribed to the Confucian way of governing a country.

Confucius and Mencius (between 5th and 4th century BC) subscribed to the belief that 'man by nature is good or kind' based on the assumption that every human is born with moral virtue. All men have an inclination to be good. In the 3rd century BC, Xunzi (the teacher of Han Fei Zi and Li Si) subscribed to the opposite belief by saying that 'man by nature is bad or evil'. He based his thought on the assumption or belief that every human is born selfish, greedy and lustful. However, Xunzi believed that man could still be made good through education. In contrast, his students, Han Fei Zi and Li Si, believed that man cannot be made good through education but state laws. To Han Fei Zi (who was a law student), the laws or legal system should be placed above the Head of State (even the Emperor). According to him, even the Emperor might behave in a selfish and greedy manner and thus the laws have to be the highest authority. If a country can put in place a proper legal system, meaning a set of well-written laws with strict enforcement, then the state will be self-regulated. Based on a review of Xunzi's and Han Fei Zi's works on Legalism, the following summary is given in Figure 3 below:

Figure 3
Conceptual Framework of Legalism

Bureaucracy
- **ranked hierarchy**
- **laws and penal code**
- **rules and regulations**
- **clear definition of what is wrong-doings**
- **systems, processes and procedures ("methodological approach")**

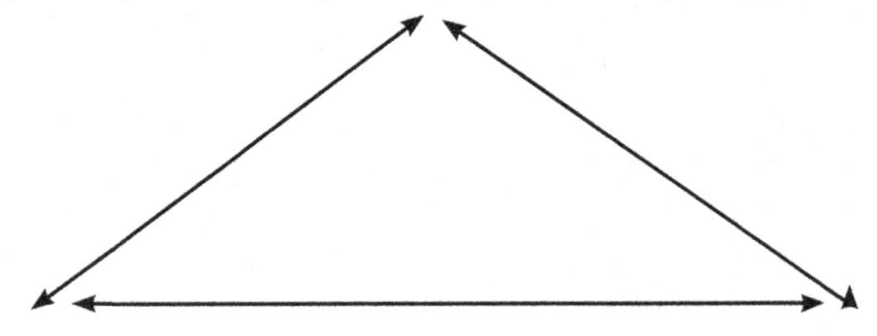

Discipline and Punishment
- **self-discipline**
- **strict enforcement**
- **no appeal process**
- **use of harsh, mean and nasty ways**

Controlled Orientation
- **Man's nature is evil and needs to be controlled**
- **use of ritual and moral principles**
- **instill fear to prevent wrongdoings**

The above framework of legalism begins with installing a comprehensive structure and system for the Court or organization. To justify any form of punishment, we need first to define what is wrongdoing. A system of justice may be designed to provide objective and impartial means for redressing those who have been wrongly accused and to punish the deserving ones. As the Chinese saying goes,

"It is far easier to reward others than to punish."

In disciplining the wrongdoer, should it be based on the rationale of 'punishment' rather than 'revenge'? Is punishment an evil act? What is the real motive or purpose of punishing? Do we punish the wrongdoer to reform him? Do we punish the wrongdoer to deter others from doing bad things? Do we punish the wrongdoer to take revenge against him? There are different views about how to treat the wrong-doer. Should one exercise more mercy for minor offences or should, everyone receive some form of punishment for their offences, regardless of whether the offences are minor or major. From ancient to contemporary times, having a penal code is unavoidable for a country, despite heavy emphasis on moral education by the government. To some extent, all governments, whether in ancient or current times, subscribe to the use of legality in governing their countries. Punishment can also be effective in teaching others. It has been said that, *"A thousand reminders is not as effective as a real punishment"*. For example, we often remind others not to speed when driving or drive recklessly as it is dangerous to oneself and others. A thousand reminders will fall on deaf ears as compared to experiencing a single accident. Once a person has an accident, it will serve as the best lesson for him or her to learn to drive cautiously in the future without endangering others.

Is it true that human nature is evil? Is it true that humans have a tendency or inclination to perform evil acts if not properly circumscribed with rules and laws? Is punishment the best way to correct the wrongdoer? To a legalist, the government is obliged to implement cruel or harsh punishments in ensuring political control and social order. To a legalist, a strict legal system with harsh punishments will strongly reinforce the authority and position or power of the ruler. If the wrongdoer is a child, is it right to smack the child for being naughty? At the family level, the average Chinese believes in disciplining his children to ensure that they will not go astray. This is why many Chinese parents keep bamboo canes at home, either to 'threaten' or 'discipline' their children in their growing up years. In many Chinese families, the mother plays the role of the compassionate one (the 'good guy' image) while the father plays the role of strict disciplinarian (the 'bad guy' image). Similarly, at an organizational level, punishing those who break the rules is unavoidable. The legalist principle of 'rule by law' is to install a legal system that functions independently in addressing any social disorder and in restoring social order. To the legalist, different periods have different problems and thus require different ways of ruling. If the rules and regulations implemented by the former king is not suitable, they need not have to be followed. Keep whatever is beneficial and change whatever is no longer relevant. That is the principle of good government.

Once an appropriate reward and punishment system are clearly spelt out and reinforced with a hierarchical structure, the legalist ruler will use a control-oriented and authoritarian style of leadership to manage the country. This is how the concept of legalism can be used to suppress any form of rebellious behavior and to restore social order and stability. For the legalist, the political system exists to serve the ruler. The emphasis is to control rather than to administer. With the right application of the system of laws supported by a bureaucratic organization and governed by a strict chain of command, the entire administration will function and regulate by itself, freeing itself from the interference of the ruler. This is the type of government or administration that the legalist ultimately would like to achieve, that is, a self-regulating system. Several of the Qin Emperors used the legalist political program and policy as a foundation in building a strong nation. This eventually led to the unification of China under legalistic rule. Based on the review of the School of Legalism of the ancient classics, I would divide Volume I of this book into 3 inter-related chapters which are:

Chapter 1: The works of Xunzi

Chapter 2: The works of Han Fei Zi

Chapter 3: A review of Chinese rulers or governments focusing on:

- 1.1 King Xuan of Qi (about 302 BC) using the works of Guan Zhong;
- 1.2 Chancellor of Qin, Shang Yang (3rd century BC) in 'the Book of Lord Shang';

1.3 Emperor Qin ShiHuang (221 – 206 BC) using the works of Han Fei Zi; and

1.4 Emperor Wu Di (141-87 BC) of the Han Dynasty who applied Confucian ideals with soft Legalist practices.

A review of the works of Xunzi and Han Fei Zi, as well as the application of the Legalist Schools of Thought of King Xuan of Qi, Shang Yang as chancellor of the Qin state, Emperor ShiHuang and his Prime Minister, Li Si during the Qin dynasty and Emperor Wu Di of the Han Dynasty provide a framework of administration for contemporary times. In Volume II, I have developed two chapters by first discussing the Western philosophy of political and legal ideologies and systems (in Chapter 4), and Chapter 5 focusing on what makes a bureaucratic organization and its relevance in today's organizational and managerial practices. In this manner, Volume I and II will provide a holistic view and the rationale for the application of the concept of legalism and the principle of bureaucracy over the past 2,500 years.

CHAPTER 1
XUNZI

Xunzi (荀子) was born with the name Xun Kuang (荀況) in 313 BC and died in 238 BC at the age of 75. Xunzi is also known as "Hsun-tsu". Although he was a Chinese Confucian philosopher, he believed that man's innate nature is evil and thus needs to be circumscribed through education and ritual. Xunzi was one of the most sophisticated thinkers of his time, and was the teacher of Li Si and Han Fei Zi. Li Si (prime minister to the first Qin emperor) and the Han state royal, Han Fei Zi developed the quasi-authoritarian aspects of Xunzi's thought into the doctrine called the School of Law, or Legalism. Xunzi's doctrines were influential in forming the official state during the Han Dynasty and the Tang Dynasty (Wikipedia, the free encyclopedia).

Xunzi's works comprise of 32 books which mainly focus on philosophy, ethics, politics and education. In contrast to Mencius's assumption that human nature is good, Xunzi holds that man is naturally inclined towards selfishness and greed, and thus needs to be curbed using the rules of law and ritual principles with a reward and punishment system. Xunzi rejects the notion that heaven is simply the natural world without a moral will as put forward by Mencius. To Xunzi, all good in society is acquired behavior and not inborn nature as claimed by Mencius. Xunzi's thoughts can be considered or classified as rationalism and realism. He subscribed to a rational and naturalistic way of looking at the universe and man. In Book 17, Xunzi described ritual as just a mechanical process, where ancestral worship or the performance of funeral rites are just an expression of grief by the living. In the same book, he commented about the question, "When people pray for rain and it rains, what does that mean? Nothing in particular, just as when people do not pray for rain, and it rains." (de Bary, 1960). To Xunzi, there is no relationship between praying for rain and the fact that it rains. To some extent, he subscribed to Lao Zi's naturalistic philosophy, seen when Xunzi commented that if one follows the "Way" closely, there is no misfortune that will happen. Lao Zi defined the "Way" as the natural laws and order that govern all creation in Nature. If one violates the "Way", Heaven cannot send a blessing. The following Table 1.1 depicts the 32 books of Xunzi:

Table 1.1
32 Books of Xunzi

Titles	
Book 1: An Exhortation to Learning	Book 17: Discourse on Nature
Book 2: On Self-Cultivation	Book 18: Rectifying Theses
Book 3: Nothing Indecorous	Book 19: Discourse on Ritual Principles
Book 4: Of Honour and Disgrace	Book 20: Discourse on Music
Book 5: Contra Physiognomy	Book 21: Dispelling Blindness
Book 6: Contra Twelve Philosophers	Book 22: On the Correct Use of Names
Book 7: On Confucius	Book 23: Man's Nature is Evil
Book 8: The Teachings of the Ru	Book 24: On the Gentleman
Book 9: On the Regulations of a King	Book 25: Working Songs
Book 10: On Enriching the State	Book 26: Fu – Rhyme – Prose Poems
Book 11: Of Kings and Lords-Protectors	Book 27: The Great Compendium
Book 12: On the Way of a Lord	Book 28: The Warning Vessel on the Right
Book 13: On the Way of Ministers	Book 29: On the Way of Sons
Book 14: On Attracting Scholars	Book 30: On the Model for Conduct
Book 15: Debate on the Principles of Warfare	Book 31: Duke Ai
Book 16: On Strengthening the State	Book 32: The Questions of Yao

Source: "Xunzi I and Xunzi II" by Library of Chinese Classics, Hunan People's Publishing House, China, 1999.

Based on an in-depth review of the above 32 books of Xunzi and the assumption made by Xunzi that man's nature is evil, this Chapter has been organized into the following seven (7) sections:

- 'Man's Nature is Evil',
- 'The Role of Ritual and Moral Principles',
- 'The Making of a Gentleman and Ruler-ship',
- 'Refinement through Learning',
- 'Ranked Hierarchy',
- 'Penal Laws and Punishments' and
- 'The Reward and Punishment System'.

To Xunzi, man's innate nature is evil, however, being a Confucian, he subscribed to the notion that man's innate nature can be corrected through ritual and moral principles, refinement through learning and self-cultivation. Besides correcting one's innate nature, Xunzi also subscribed to the use of rules and regulations as well as penal laws and punishments to circumscribe one's conduct of behavior. He discussed extensively in his works the difference between the capable and the incapable, as well as the making of a gentleman and a wise ruler. He strongly emphasized that for a state to operate in an orderly way, it comes down to the ability of a ruler to assemble its officials (from the prime minister to the lowest officials) by designing and installing a properly ranked hierarchy with well-defined roles, responsibilities and duties. Besides this, Xunzi distinguished humans from other beings by saying that humans are born with a thinking faculty and a high level of awareness or consciousness. In Book 9.19, Xunzi said, *"Fire and water possess vital breath but have no life. Plants and trees possess life, but lack awareness. Birds and beasts have awareness, but lack a sense of morality and justice. Humans possess vital breath, life, and awareness, and add to them a sense of morality and justice. It is for this reason that they are the noblest beings in the world..."* Only humans can form societies –with different divisions and classes – subsequently reinforced by the moral and ethical behavior of its people. If every individual acts according to his social division and class, unity will result, and order, harmony and prosperity will follow. The following Figure 1.1 depicts the layout of Chapter 1.

Figure 1.1
Conceptual Framework of Xunzi

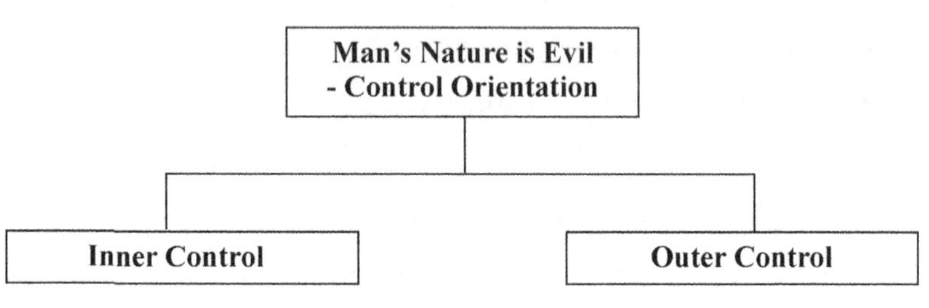

Inner Control
- The Role of Ritual and Moral Principles
- The Making of a Gentleman and Rulership
- Refinement through Education

Outer Control
- Ranked Hierarchy
- Penal Laws and Punishments
- The Reward and Punishment System

The above framework is conceptualized based on a two-factor theory or concept where the 'outer control' serves as prevention from doing evil actions while the 'inner control' serves as a way to cultivate good deeds. Not doing evil things is different from doing good deeds. As a responsible person, it is a minimum requirement not to do anything harmful to others or the environment. Once this can be achieved, then a person should strive to do good deeds. Xunzi believed in man's nature, from the ability to avoid doing evil to cultivating the desire to do good deeds. Xunzi's ultimate goal was to transmute and transform man. As he described in Book 3.9, the **"Power of Nature"** is the ability to transmute and transform. As man evolves from Nature, he should also possess this ability.

Man's Nature is Evil

Xunzi's primary assumption about man is that man's nature is evil. In Book 23.2, Xunzi said,
"Now, the nature of man is such that he is born with a love of profit.

Following this nature will cause its aggressiveness and greedy tendencies to grow and courtesy and deference to disappear. Humans are born with feelings of envy and hatred. Indulging these feelings causes violence and crime to develop and loyalty and trustworthiness to perish. Man is born possessing the desires of the ears and eyes (which are fond of sounds and colors). Indulging these desires causes dissolute and wanton behaviour to result and ritual and moral principles, precepts of good form, and the natural order of reason to perish.

This being the case, when each person follows his inborn nature and indulges his natural inclinations, aggressiveness and greed are certain to develop. This is accompanied by violation of social class distinctions and throws the natural order into anarchy, resulting in a cruel tyranny. Thus, it is necessary that man's nature undergo the transforming influence of a teacher and the model and that he be guided by ritual and moral principles. Only after this has been accomplished do courtesy and deference develop. Unite these qualities with precepts of good form and reason, and the result is an age of orderly government. If we consider the implications of these facts, it is plain that human nature is evil and that any good in humans is acquired by conscious exertion." (Knoblock, 1999).

To Xunzi, the roots of a man's evil nature are his selfishness and greed. If a man is driven by his evil nature, all types of evil acts will result such as theft, cheating and exploiting others in exchange for personal gain. The Chinese classify these behaviors as the act of a 'petty man'. On the other hand, if a man is driven by his good nature, he will conduct his behavior ethically, such as being generous and compassionate to others – the acts of a 'gentleman'. He will not cause harm to others. Based on the assumption that man's nature is evil, in order to move people onto the right path, it is essential to:

(a) Institutionalize a set of ritual and moral principles;

(b) Emphasize the importance of studying and the role of a teacher; and

(c) Develop and implement a penal law and punishment system.

In the 32 chapters of Xunzi, he confined much of his discussion to the above three essentials or fundamentals of the making of a man. Xunzi asserted that man will not show deference to others unless he or she is guided by the right ritual and moral principles learnt from the Sage. In Book 23.6, Xunzi described the inborn nature of man who when hungry desires something to eat, when cold wants warm clothing, and when weary desires rest (Knoblock, 1999). These are examples of man's natural behavior and it is unlikely that he will show deference to others. If you want a human to do good, it has to be acquired through conscious exertion.

When someone asked Xunzi how men would develop those stated ritual and moral principles since man's nature is evil, Xunzi replied that the ritual and moral principles can be developed from the Sage. The Sage, through earnest learning and practice, transformed his original nature into an acquired nature. Once he developed those ritual principles and moral duty, he could institutionalize them. As argued by Xunzi (in Book 23.7), man's love of profit and desire to obtain material wealth is natural. Suppose that two brothers obtained valuable goods. Without the guidance of proper ritual and moral principles, both brothers will fight among themselves over the wealth. However, with the guidance of proper ritual and moral principles, they will transform themselves and be willing to share the valuable goods with each other. If it is based on inborn nature, man will naturally fight for what they naturally desire and would not understand the importance of deference to others.

In Book 23.8, Xunzi further asserted that if man is not properly circumscribed by ritual and moral principles, he will act in a rebellious and perverse manner, which conforms to his original innate behavior. Just as natural materials like wood can be steamed to soften them and then forced to bend into a required shape, man's behavior must also be transformed and then further refined through education and learned behavior. This is the power of learning. The ultimate purpose of learning is to change, and the theory of learning is equal to the theory of change. In Book 28.12, Xunzi discussed man's ability to learn and to change. Although man's nature is evil, it is also man's inborn nature that possesses the natural ability to acquire moral principles, study them, and through earnest practice transform his or her inborn nature into acquired nature. In this sense, it justifies the role of a wise ruler or Sage in making the transformation into a reality. Thus, a related assumption about man is, besides his nature being evil, man also possesses the ability to change his nature. The outcome of learning is **CHANGE**. It is through earnest learning and practice that one might change one's nature and cultivate oneself to become a gentleman. Thus, the main purpose of learning is to change.

The Principle of Learning = The Principle of Change

The Role of Ritual and Moral Principles

To Xunzi (in Book 4.11), all men possess the same natural needs; when hungry, they desire food; when cold, they desire to warmth; when exhausted, they desire rest; and they all desire benefit and hate being harmed. In addition, all men are born with certain inborn abilities; the eye distinguishes white from black, the beautiful from the ugly. The ear distinguishes sounds and tones as to their shrillness or sonority. The mouth distinguishes the sour and salty, the sweet and bitter. The nose distinguishes perfumes and fragrances, rancid and fetid odors. The bones, flesh, and skin-lines distinguish hot and cold, pain and itching (Knoblock, 1999). Man is born with natural desires for food, warmth and shelter. If a man is not properly regulated by ritual and moral principles, he will be easily overcome by his own desires. In Book 19, Xunzi explained that if a man acts with only profit in mind, loss is certain. Similarly, if a man seeks happiness through self-gratification, destruction is certain. If a man fully follows ritual and moral principles in pursuing his desires, he will be able to enjoy real happiness.

Whether a man becomes good or bad largely depends on the

environment or circumstances, as well as the influence of rituals and customs. Based on Xunzi's observation and understanding, many people become the latter while only a few belong to the former. The inborn nature of man has an inclination to be petty – selfish and greedy. If a person is brought up without a good teacher to guide them on the principles of humanity and justice as well as moral values, he or she will naturally see things solely in terms of benefit to self. It is only through earnest cultivation and conscious exertion that one can become a gentleman and be wise. If the population of the world lacks proper cultivation, it will turn out to be the greatest calamity for man. Even 25 centuries after Xunzi's death, the world in which we live is still lacking in the desired type of moral values.

In today's so-called civilized society, there is still a high proportion of people who belong to the inferior type. The importance of circumscribing human conduct with ritual and moral principles has never been less emphasized. A society should continuously move people from the inferior order to the middle order, and ultimately to the highest order. As stated in Book 24. 2, when someone makes a mistake, he will voluntarily acknowledge his offences. This is the kind of gracious society that most people yearn to live in., it is important to ensure that throughout man's civilization, future generations are better than current and past generations. Xunzi categorized the young people of his time into three groups (in Book 2.12):

Good youth - someone who is straightforward and diligent, obedient and respectful of his elders.

Despicable youth - someone who is evasive, timorous, and shirks his duties, coupled with the lack of any sense of modesty or shame and has an inordinate fondness for food and drink.

Ill-omened youth - someone who possesses the bad qualities of a despicable youth as well as profligacy, cruelty, disobedience, treachery, malice and disrespectful to others.

At times we lament that the future generations are worse than our past and present generations. However, we must not forget that we are also responsible for shaping and nurturing the next generations. If they are getting worse, we should be held responsible. It is important for a country to devote more resources to educating our youth, especially in the cultivation of humanity, justice and moral values. Then we can be assured that the next generation will be better than ours. In defining ritual and moral principles, Xunzi stated in book 27.104,

"Humanity, morality, ritual principles, and goodness belong in man the way valuables, goods, grain, and rice belong in the household. Those that have them in abundance are rich: those that have them in small quantities are poor. To be entirely without them is to be utterly impoverished. Thus, for the great to be incapable and the small to fail to act is the Way to abandon the state and damage the self." In book 27.24, Xunzi reiterated the importance of rituals by saying, *"Ritual principles provide the footing men tread on. When men lose this footing, they stumble and fall, sink and drown. When observance of small matters is neglected, the disorder that results is great. Such is ritual."* (Knoblock, 1999).

To a large extent, Xunzi possessed similar thoughts as Confucius by using ritual and moral principles to circumscribe the people's behavior in ensuring social harmony and political order. On the other hand, Xunzi also discussed the consequences of not having rituals. In his book 27.33, Xunzi said,

"Where ritual is not obtained, between lord and minister there is no honoured position, between father and son is no affection; between elder and younger brother no submissiveness, and between husband and wife no rejoicing. Through it, the young grow to maturity, and the old acquire nourishment. Thus Heaven and Earth produce it and the sage perfects it." (Knoblock, 1999).

In discussing the duality between **a sense of rightness** versus **a sense of profits**, Xunzi said,

"..... When superiors stress the importance of morality, morality overcomes profit; when they stress profit, then profit overcomes morality. Thus, the Son of Heaven does not discuss quantities, feudal lords do not discuss benefit and harm, grand officers do not discuss success and failure, and knights do not discuss commerce and merchandise." (Book 27.67 of Xunzi, Knoblock, 1999).

The key principle of a gentleman is where:

A sense of rightness/morality > A sense of profits

If a person's sense of profits is more than his sense of rightness (knowing what is right and what is wrong), then he will resort to unscrupulous means in getting what he wants. If a person's sense of rightness is more than his sense of profits, then he will conduct himself morally and will not cause harm to others. In the discussion between the duality of rightness and profits, Xunzi (in book 27.70) said, *"When superiors love moral conduct, then the people conduct themselves in a refined manner even in private. When superiors love wealth, then the people are willing to die for profits..."* (Knoblock, 1999). The relationship between rightness and profits is similar to 'trust and loyalty' between the leader and his subordinates. If a leader trusts his subordinates, his subordinates will automatically be loyal to him for a long time. Besides this, a wise leader needs to provide correct examples through his actions in order for his subordinates to emulate them. In contemporary times, we call this **"Leadership by Example"**. If a leader provides a good example, others will behave well. If a leader provides a bad/poor example, others will also follow suit.

If the gentleman is able to rid himself of any consideration of profit at the cost of morality, shame and disgrace will never come (Book 30.3 of Xunzi). A wise ruler knows men and employs worthy and upright people to serve the country. Use the worthy and upright people to reform the unworthy and it will cause perverse and petty men to be transformed. As Xunzi said, "*.... Ritual was created on* *behalf of men from worthies down to the ordinary masses.."* (Book 27.14, Knoblock, 1999). As Xunzi reiterated in book 27.11, if a ruler establishes a humane heart within himself, ritual will follow and be put into practice. It is only when rituals have been put into practice that men will treat each other appropriately and with respect. All human beings desire and seek out relationships with others to satisfy their need for affiliation through interpersonal interactions. In fact, a successful career, family, and friendships to a large extent depend on maintaining good inter-relationship with others. To Xunzi, humane behavior is the manifestation of love, and morality is the manifestation of natural order. In contemporary times, it has been said that out of three successful people, it can be safely said that two of them possess good interpersonal relationships with others while the other one's success is based on capability. If we study a happy person, it can be deduced that some 80% of his or her happiness is derived from their good interpersonal relationships with others. This means that good interpersonal relationships with others account for over 80% of our happiness index. Similarly in an organization, a wise leader is not only well-behaved but systematically diffuses and inculcates the right conduct among his or her followers. Proper conduct or behavior is the fundamental principle for all harmonious relationships.

In governing a State, Xunzi (in Book 16.2) said,

".... When rites and music are reformed and cultivated, when social divisions and the obligations congruent with them are kept clear, when promotions and demotions are timely, when a love for the people and a desire to benefit them is given visible form...............

Rites and music are not kept in good order; social divisions and their inherent obligations are not kept clear; promotions and demotions are not timely; a love for the people and a desire to benefit them is not given visible form......." (Knoblock, 1999).

This is how Xunzi subscribed to the importance of rites and rituals in the development of an orderly and harmonious society. To

Xunzi, *"It is through ritual that the individual is rectified. It is by means of a teacher that ritual is rectified. If there were no rituals, how could the individual be rectified? If there were no teachers, how could you know which ritual is correct? ......* (Book 2.11, Knoblock, 1999). Xunzi emphasized on the importance of learning and the role of a teacher in regulating and shaping the behavior of the people. The role of a teacher is to transmit the ritual and moral principles of the ancient times to the young and to future generations. Confucius's and Xunzi's time was one of decorum that emphasized on the proper code of conduct of an educated and civilized person. Book 2.7 of Xunzi discussed what constitutes a person of proper conduct.

"He does not walk with his hands folded respectfully before him because he fears that he may soil his sleeves in the mud. Nor does he walk with his head bowed because he is worried that he may collide with something. He is not the first to lower his eyes when he encounters a colleague out of fear and trepidation. The scholar behaves in this way because he desires only to cultivate his own person and incur no blame from the common folk of his neighbourhood." (Knoblock, 1999)

If an individual learns and practices the good conduct of behavior from a young age, when he matures, he will know to treat others well with humaneness. That explains why many teachers and philosophers of ancient China emphasized the teaching of proper ritual and moral principles as the basic study for all primary education. In Book 4.1 and 4.2, Xunzi discussed the importance of having a code of conduct in circumscribing one's behavior and interpersonal relationships. In Book 4.1, Xunzi said, *"Pride and excess bring disaster for man. Respectfulness and moderation ward off the five weapons, for although the lance and spear are piercing, they are not so sharp as respectfulness and moderation. Hence, words of praise for another are warmer than clothing of linen and silk. The wound caused by words is deeper than that of spears and halberds. ...."* The importance of effective communication and interpersonal relationships is not less emphasized in today's digital age. Although information technology has enabled individuals to communicate better and faster, much of our interpersonal conflicts are due to ineffective and poor communication that causes breakdown. The key reason is the way we communicate. It is the **manner** that makes a person. The emphasis on mannerisms or 'behaving yourself well' has to be emphasized from young, especially within the family. Xunzi further added (in Book 4.2) that,

"For all their cheerfulness, they perish because of their anger. For all their careful investigations, they are destroyed by their viciousness. For all their breadth of knowledge, they are reduced to poverty because of their penchant for slander. For all their appearance of personal probity, they sink further into corruption because they revile others. For all the fine foods they eat, they become even more emaciated because they associate indiscriminately. For all their discriminations, they do not provide convincing explanations because they are interested only in debate. ....." (Knoblock, 1999).

Again the importance of a proper code of conduct with a high practice of "Emotional Quotient" (EQ) in interpersonal relationships has been emphasized in our social networking. In many western cross-cultural studies, the average Chinese is known to belong to the 'high-context in communication style' category which means in communication, the Chinese tends to be implicit, indirect and subtle. At times, in communication, the Chinese would rather hide the truth than embarrass others. In rejecting others, the Chinese avoid saying **"NO"** directly as that would embarrass the counterpart. Like the Japanese, the Chinese have several ways to say "NO" indirectly such as "I will let you know later", Let me think about it" or "It is a good proposal but ....".

In many ways, our behaviors are defined and shaped by the environment, especially the kind of friends we associated with. As Xunzi pointed out in his Book 23.19, if a person is surrounded by bad people or friends, he will be exposed to hearing words of deception, treachery and hypocrisy. Each day, he will see reckless, wanton, wicked and greedy acts. Consciously and unconsciously, he will be influenced by evil and do disgraceful things. On the other hand, if a person is surrounded by good and nice people, his conduct of behavior will be marked by loyalty, trust, respect and politeness. Gradually, he will advance in humaneness and morality and be a good citizen. As Xunzi said, *"If you do not understand your son, look at his friends. If you do not understand your lord, look at the people serving him."* As the saying goes, choosing a friend is like choosing a lifestyle.

Throughout the Chinese dynastic system of over 2,000 years, all rulers understood the importance of elevating the worthy and promoting those with moral worth. In this manner, a country will be well-ordered. In contemporary times, organizations need to be managed by people of capability and of high integrity as per Figure 1.1.

Figure 1.1
Capability and Integrity

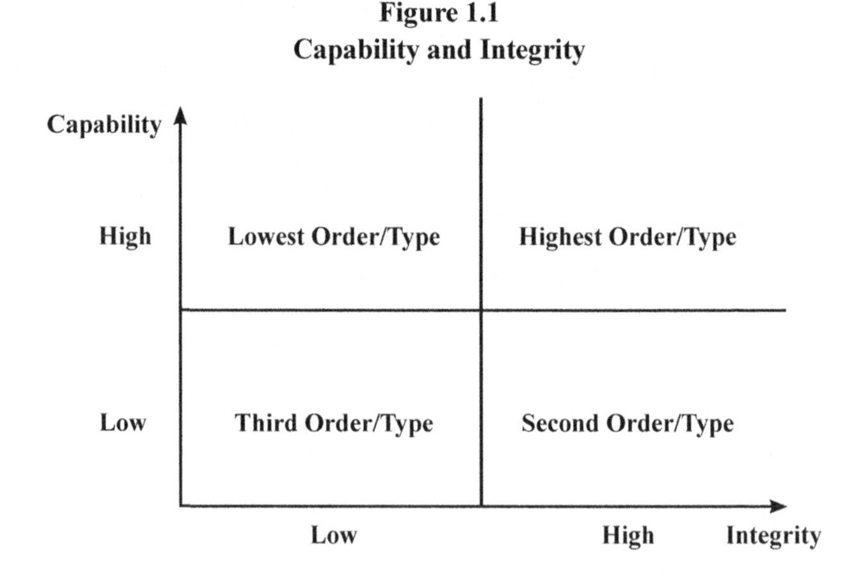

Based on Figure 1.1, employees with high capability and high integrity will be classified as the Highest Order of Employees. Employees with high integrity but low capability will be ranked as the Second Order of Employees. However, in ranking the third and lowest order of employees, employees with High Capability but

Low Integrity were ranked as the lowest order of employees. This is because, if a person possesses high capability but is low in integrity, he or she is capable of creating 'trouble' in an organization. Thus, it is not advisable to employ someone who is capable but has a gross lack of integrity. If you are not careful, these people can bring more 'harm' than 'good' to the organization as they have the capability to do so. On the other hand, an employee who is low in both capability and integrity is less harmful and thus ranked in the third order.

In contemporary times, a wise leader should determine a person's character first before he determines his capability. A person's performance depends more on the outcome of a person's work attitude (his character) than a person's work capability. If a person lacks capability but possesses a good work attitude, he will work extra hard to obtain a better performance. On the other hand, if a person has high capability but has a poor work attitude, he will refrain from contributing effectively. Thus, the character of a person should be established first before determining his capability.

In book 31.6 of Xunzi, Duke Ai questioned Confucius on the criteria of choosing or selecting someone. Based on Confucius's reply, there are three types of people that one should refrain from, namely clever, glib and talkative men. To Confucius, a clever man is covetous and a glib man will create disorder and confusion, as a glib man speaks without sincerity, whereas a talkative man is unreliable in his speech. In selecting someone, we must first determine or prove his trustworthiness. It is only once his trustworthiness has been ascertained that we can seek to determine his knowledge and ability. A person who possesses knowledge and ability but lacks trustworthiness is likened to a wolf.

For most Chinese managers or leaders, if power is given to a gentleman, he will use it wisely and use it to benefit the people and the organization. On the other hand, if power is given to a petty man, he will abuse it and use it for his own benefit at the expense of the organization. Power itself is neither good nor bad (neutral). It lies with the people using it. Just like a knife, it can be used as a tool to cut food. It can also be used as a weapon to kill others. There are two sides to the same coin.

With respect to ritual and moral principles, Xunzi placed great importance on self-cultivation in establishing oneself. To Xunzi (in Book 2), man has the innate nature to preserve within himself what he sees as good. When a man finds what is good within himself, he will find ways to cherish it. When he sees what is not good within himself, his teachers will correct him. In Book 2.2, Xunzi described a 'gentleman' as someone who continuously cultivated his character and strengthened his reputation. He subscribed to self-cultivation as a means for one to measure oneself against the ritual principles and being trustworthy. To Xunzi, a cultured person will always abide or even exceed the ritual principles. Or else one will be seen as arrogant and obstinate, depraved and perverted, utterly commonplace and savage (Knoblock, 1999). In Book 2.4, Xunzi provided a comprehensive write up on how to control one's vital breath and nourish the mind, as follows:

"If the blood humour is too strong and robust, calm it with balance and harmony.
If knowledge and foresight are too penetrating and deep, unify them with ease and
sincerity.
If the impulse to daring bravery is too fierce and violent, stay it with guidance and
instruction.
If the quickness of the mind and the fluency of the tongue are too punctilious and sharp,
moderate them in your activity and rest.........
Truly this procedure may properly be called 'the method of controlling the vital breath
and nourishing the mind.'" (Knoblock, 1999)

In cultivating oneself, Xunzi subscribed to the concept of

moderation or the principle of 'Zhong Yong' as espoused by Confucius. To Confucius and Xunzi, moderation in opinion and conduct is a well-known distinguishing characteristic of the true gentleman. The gentleman avoids the absolute and the extreme - having too much is as bad as having too little – the philosophy of compromise. If a person practices moderation, he subscribes to central harmony, which emphasizes the practice of moderation by avoiding the practice of extremes. It focuses on the middle way of human thought and action, and thus becomes an important principle for people to observe and earnestly practice.

The "Virtue of Moderation" is the highest wisdom of all humankind. It is easy to follow but difficult to master. In whatever we do, if we overdo it, things will go back to square one. To keep to the moderate would be the best advice. Everything can be defined by its opposite, thus it is important for one not to let things develop to extremes. This is an important piece of wisdom that people need to observe and practice. By allowing things to stretch to extremes, misery will follow. To Xunzi (as stated in Book 2.4), if one expresses himself to the extreme such as when one's blood humor is **too** strong and robust, knowledge and foresight are **too** penetrating and deep, or the quickness of the mind and the fluency of the tongue are **too** punctilious and sharp, it brings about bad consequences. To the Chinese, the principle of 'moderation' is the Chinese version of EQ (Emotional Quotient) – the Chinese EQ. EQ can be defined as knowing your own feelings and possessing the ability to manage them. Human emotions are the domain of core feelings, gut level instincts and emotional sensations. The human heart radiates and activates our deepest values, transforming them from something we think about to what we live. Be sensitive and confident when interacting with others. Develop a proactive personality and expression.

"Do not be over-sensitive when interacting with others.

Do not impose your will and try to dominate others."

The Making of a Gentleman and Ruler-ship

As a Confucian scholar, Xunzi differentiated man into two categories that are the 'gentleman' and the 'inferior/petty man'. In Book 17, Xunzi described a gentleman as someone who develops what is within his power rather than derives his power from Heaven, while the petty man seeks what comes from Heaven instead of what is within his power. Thus, the gentleman progresses each day while the petty man degenerates daily (de Bary, 1960). Xunzi basically categorized bravery into three orders or types (Book 23.18) where:

- a person is said to be of the highest order or type if he holds oneself straight and upright; he carries out his ideals in practice; he is not bothered with material wealth; and he possesses the desire to share with others.
- a person is said to be of the middle order or type if he is respectful in ritual conduct and modest in his ideas; he attaches high importance to purifying himself and personal integrity; and he considers material wealth trivial.
- a person is said to be of the inferior order or type if he places no importance to hiss own character while placing great importance to material wealth; he remains complacent during calamity and attempts to avoid blame; he disregards what is right or wrong; and he enjoys the fruits of others' ideas to benefit himself.

In Book 30.8, Xunzi cited Confucius, stating that a gentleman should reflect on three matters, which are when he is young, he must study hard, when he has matured he must teach others and when he possesses things, he must learn to share them with others. If a person does not study when he is young, he will have no abilities when he matures. If a person does not teach when he matures, no one will reflect on his life when he dies. If a person does not share when he has things, no one will share with him when he is in difficulty (Knoblock, 1999). In Book 2.3, Xunzi discussed the character and behavior contrast between a gentleman and a petty man (inferior man) as:

"To lead others with what is good is called 'education.' To agree with others for the sake of what is good is called 'concord.' To lead others with what is not good is called 'flattery.' To agree with others in the interests of what is not good is called 'toadying.' To recognize as right what is right and as wrong what is wrong is called 'wisdom.' To regard as wrong what is right and as right what is wrong is called 'stupidity.' 'Slander' is doing injury to an honourable man; 'malefaction' is doing him harm. 'Straightforwardness' is calling right what is right and wrong what is wrong. 'Robbery' is stealing property; 'deceit' is concealing conduct; and 'boasting' is treating words lightly. One whose inclinations and aversions are unsettled is called 'inconstant.' One who protects personal profit at the expense of abandoning his moral duty is called 'utterly malicious.' One who has heard much is 'broad'; one who has heard little is 'shallow.' One who has seen much is 'cultivated'; one who has seen little is 'provincial.' He who has difficulty obtaining advancement in office is 'dilatory'; and he who easily forgets is 'oblivious.' One who, though he does only a few things, obeys natural principles in organizing what he does is 'well ordered'; one who, though he does many things, lacks any principle of organization in what he does is 'bewildered.'" (Knoblock, 1999).

In this book, Xunzi highlighted more than ten differences between a gentleman and petty man (an inferior man). If a person is guided by his good nature, he will become a gentleman. If a person is guided by his bad nature, he will become a petty man. After birth, a person's character and behavior is not just determined by his nature but rather nurture. Thus, the making of a person depends on his learning, socialization process and the environment. In Book 2.5, Xunzi added,

"........ The gentleman works external things: the petty man works for external things. Do whatever causes the mind to be serene though it gives the body toil, and whatever causes one's sense for what is right to develop, though it diminishes the concern for profit. Serving a disruptive lord and being successful is not as good as serving an impoverished lord and being obedient in such service. ...." (Knoblock, 1999).

Through self-cultivation and the earnest practice of ritual and moral principles, one is capable of becoming a cultured man that possesses the qualities of a gentleman. In defining a gentleman's qualities, Xunzi said (Book 2.15),

"In times of hardship and poverty, the gentleman broadens his sense of purpose. In times of prosperity and honour, he comports himself with respectfulness. When tranquil and at ease, his blood humour is not enfeebled. In times of fatigue and exhaustion, his appearance is not slovenly. He does not commit the excess of snatching things back out of anger or that of giving things away out of joy. The gentleman can broaden his sense of purpose even in times of hardship and poverty because he exalts the principle of humanity. He is able to comport himself with respectfulness toward others even when he is wealthy and honoured because he deprecates the power and influence that accompany them. ...... " (Knoblock, 1999).

For thousands of years, the average Chinese has had an ultimate goal in life which is to make a good name or reputation for himself in order to glorify his past ancestors and current family-name. That is why it is crucial for one to cultivate oneself and become a true gentleman. In explaining the consequences of being a gentleman and a petty man, Xunzi (in book 4.9) said,

"....... The petty man is eager to make boasts, yet desires that others should believe in him. He enthusiastically engages in deception, yet wants others to have affection for him. He conducts himself like an animal, yet wants others to think well of him. When he reflects on something, it is understood only with difficulty. When he acts in regard to something, it is difficult for him to make it secure. When he tries to sustain something, he has difficulty establishing it. In the end, he is certain to fail to obtain what he loves and sure to encounter what he hates.

Accordingly, the gentleman is trustworthy and so desires that other men should trust him as well. He is loyal and so wants other

men to have affection for him. He cultivates rectitude and makes orderly his management of the situation, and so desires that others should think well of him. When he reflects on something, it is easily understood. When he acts, it is easy for him to make it secure. When he tries to sustain something, it is easily established. In the end, he is certain to obtain what he loves and sure not to encounter what he hates. For these reasons, when he is unsuccessful in seeking office, he will not live in obscurity; when he is successful, he will become greatly illustrious; and when he dies, his reputation will be still more extensively declared….." (Knoblock, 1999).

As the average Chinese believes, it is the **character of a person** that determines the destiny of a man. Thus, it is important to cultivate one's character before one can actualize what he or she wants. In respect of character versus capability/competency, Xunzi put higher emphasis on character before capability/competency. The cultivating of character is primary in the development of a gentleman or a ruler. In Book 12.4, Xunzi cited, *"The ruler is the sundial; the people are the shadow. If the form is upright, then the shadow will be upright. The ruler is the bowl; the people the water. If the bowl is round, then the water will be round; if it is square, then the water will be square…"* (Knoblock, 1999). To Xunzi, leadership and followership define each other. In contemporary times, many leadership development courses emphasize on **"Leadership by Example"** - where the followers' behavior is the mirror-image of their leaders.

Defining the capability of a gentleman does not mean that the gentleman has to be all-knowing and all-capable. In Book 8.5 of Xunzi, he said, *"When the gentleman is termed "worthy", this does not mean that he is capable of all that able men can do. When he is termed "wise", this does not imply that he can know all that knowledgeable men know. When he is termed "discriminating", this does not mean that he is able to discriminate all that dialecticians can discriminate…."* (Knoblock, 1999). All men have their limitations. A scholar may be good at the classics but when compared to a trader, he will be inferior in evaluating the value of a product and the modus operandi of a market. As knowledge is unlimited while the life of an individual is limited, what one knows will be insignificant when compared to what one does not know. A wise leader understands this and will moderate his expectations of his subordinates.

In Book 5, Xunzi described , the King as likely to be ashamed to have petty men as ministers; a father would be ashamed to have them as sons; the average man would be ashamed to have them as friends; and so on. For thousands of years, the average Chinese family felt shameful to have a child who committed evil deeds such as theft, cheating or committing any form of crime. In some families, the parents would even disown their children for bringing too much shame to the family. In describing the three bad characteristics of a petty man, Xunzi said (Book 5.8):

- when he occupies a superior position, he is unable to love those below him;

- in front of others, he appears agreeable but behind their back, he insults them; and

- he is unable to distinguish between crookedness and uprightness and unable to attract capable and wise people to work for him.

In Book 6.5, Xunzi further described a petty man as someone who honors the principle of the law but himself acts as though there is no law. The gentleman and the petty man are opposites. Table 1.1 depicts some of the differences highlighted by Xunzi in Book 3.3, 3.6 and 3.12 as follows:

Table 1.1
The Distinction between the Gentleman and the Petty Man

The Gentleman	The Petty Man
- If the gentleman has ability, he is magnanimous, generous, tolerant, and straightforward.	- If the petty man is capable, he is rude and arrogant, perverted and depraved.
- If he is incapable, he is respectful, reverent, moderate, and modest.	- If the petty man is incapable, he is envious, jealous, resentful and given to backbiting, so that he subverts and undermines others.
- When the gentleman is bold of heart, he reveres Heaven and follows its Way.	- When the petty man is bold of heart, he is indolent and haughty.
- When faint of heart, he is awe-inspired by his sense of moral duty and regulates his conduct to accord with it.	- When faint of heart, he drifts into lechery and is subversive.
- When knowledgeable, he understands the interconnections between phenomena and can assign them to their proper logical category.	- When knowledgeable, he is predatory and clandestine.
- When ignorant, he is honest and diligent and can follow the model.	- When ignorant, he is poisonously malicious and given to rebelliousness.
- When he is happy, he is concordant with others and well-ordered in his person.	- When he is happy, he is frivolous and flighty.
- When saddened, he maintains inner quietude and preserves his distinctive qualities.	- When saddened, he is crushed and despondent.
- If he meets with success, he maintains good form and makes it illustrious.	- If he meets with success, he is filled with pride and is unfair.
- If he encounters hardship, he is frugal and proceeds with care.	- If he encounters hardship, he becomes negligent and unambitious.
The gentleman doubly advances: - Public-spiritedness produces clear understanding; - Straightforwardness and diligence produce success; and - Sincerity and honesty produce perspicacity.	The petty man doubly regresses: - Partisanship produces dark obscurity; - Deceitfulness and falsity produce obstructions; and - Boastfulness and bragging produce self-delusion.

Source: "Xunzi", Library of Chinese Classics, Hunan People's Publishing House, Foreign Languages Press, China" translated by John Knoblock, 1999.

In terms of people management, a gentleman supervisor will use the strengths or the good nature of his people such as:

- integrity/righteousness/courage of his people in conducting his business;
- humanism/benevolence/compassion of his people in dealing with his stakeholders such as the employees, suppliers, customers, bankers and the community at large;
- determination/confidence/self-esteem of his people to achieve a higher level of excellence without compromise or the use of unscrupulous means; and
- patience/perseverance/calmness/coolness of his people in dealing with low periods or crisis.

On the other hand, a petty supervisor will only use the weaknesses or the bad nature of man to do evil things such as:

- selfishness/self-centeredness of his people to work hard for personal interest at the expense of his work colleagues;
- greed (fame/power/wealth) of his people to exploit others;
- deceptiveness (lie/cheat) of his people to take advantage of his stakeholders such as his employees, suppliers, customers, bankers and the community at large; and
- the bad temper of his people to act on impulse to do courageous act that lack integrity.

In many Chinese classics, much has been discussed of the differences between the gentleman and the inferior/petty man. In contemporary times, there is no empirical evidence to say what percentage of the people in the society belongs to the gentleman and petty man categories. The numbers vary from time to time, and from society to society. In making a further distinction between the gentleman and the petty man, Xunzi defined the differences between what is honorable and what is disgraceful. In book 4.7, he wrote "*.... Those who put first what is just and later matters of benefit are* *honorable; those who put first what is beneficial and later what is just are shameful. Those who are honorable always gain success; those who are shameful invariably fail. The successful always administer others; failures are always administered by others. Such is the great distinction between honor and disgrace……."* (Knoblock, 1999). This explains why Chinese culture is normally known as a shame culture while Western culture is normally referred to as a guilt culture. Shame culture can be defined as a culture with a sense of shame that encourages one to exercise high self-discipline. Guilt-culture is defined as culture with a sense of guilt that deters one from committing wrong-doing.

Besides making distinction between the characteristics and behavior of a gentleman and a petty man, Xunzi discussed much on the qualities of a gentleman in Book 3.2, 3.4 and 3.5 (Knoblock, 1999). Xunzi described a gentleman as someone who is:

- easily made apprehensive but is difficult to intimidate
- dreads suffering but will not avoid what is required by his moral duty, even at the risk of death
- desirous of what is beneficial but will not do what is wrong
- considerate but not partial

Being a Confucian, Xunzi subscribed to the principle of moderation (the Principle of **"Zhong Yong" or "The Mean" /"中 庸"** espoused by Confucius). When asked to explain what is humaneness, Xunzi defined this in his Book 5.9 as someone who knows how to draw boundaries. To Xunzi, men are born with natural desires such as to eat when hungry, to wear clothes when cold, to sleep when tired and to desire what is beneficial and avoid what is harmful. However, in fulfilling one's desires, a gentleman knows how to observe moderation and thus avoid any form of excessiveness. In Book 3, Xunzi further stated that:

- He is magnanimous, but not to the point of being remiss.
- He is scrupulous but not to the point of inflicting suffering.

- He engages in argumentation but not to the point of causing a quarrel.
- He is critical but not to the point of provoking others.
- When he upholds an upright position, he is not haughty. While flexible and tractable, he does not merely drift with the demands of the occasion. He bends and unbends as the occasion demands and he is flexible and tractable like the rushes and reeds, not because of fear and cowardice. He is able to employ his sense of what is morally right to bend or straighten, changing and responding to suit every occasion.

In Book 7.3, Xunzi described a true gentleman as someone who develops what is highest and most noble and thus, is able to win the hearts and minds of men. On the other hand, if a man uses stratagems and tactics and then judges the efforts and slackness of his men to bring down his enemies, he is not a true gentleman. As a true gentleman (in Book 17.4), one must be able to do the following:

- Being the worthiest of men, they are able to help the unworthy.
- Being the strongest of men, they are able to be magnanimous toward the weak.

In Book 19, Xunzi discussed the role of a ruler in the development of a nation. To Xunzi, a ruler is in the most influential position of authority and responsible for the prosperity or misery of a nation. A truly wise ruler must possess the moral force to establish justice and trust among the people. In defining what constitutes a wise ruler, Xunzi (in Book 11.9) states that:

"Those who are to maintain the state certainly cannot do so alone. Since this is the case, the strength, defensive security, and glory of a country lie in the selection of its prime minister. Where a ruler is himself able and his prime minister is able, he will become a True King. Where the ruler is personally incapable, but knows it, becomes apprehensive, and seeks those who are able, then he will become powerful. When the ruler is personally incapable, but neither realizes

it, nor becomes apprehensive, nor seeks those who are able, but merely makes use of those who fawn over him and flatter him, those who form his entourage of assistants, or those who are related to him, then he will be endangered and encroached upon, and, in the extreme case, annihilated... " (Knoblock, 1999).

A wise ruler not only practices a high degree of humanity by placing moral duty first, but he must be able and capable in executing his duty. An able ruler can engage able people and in return cause other able men to act on his behalf. He must be capable of using worthy means and exercise a high degree of discretion by using what is important for significant matters. A wise ruler must first put his country in a state of good order before pursuing personal pleasure. In respect of rulership, Xunzi further pointed out in Book 9.1 that a wise ruler should:

- Promote worthy and capable people without regard to seniority;
- Dismiss the unfit and incapable without hesitation;
- Execute evildoers; and
- Transform the multitude.

As stated in Book 9.2 of Xunzi, a wise ruler should possess the ability to clearly distinguish between the worthy and unworthy; the right and the wrong. In his daily conduct, a wise ruler should adopt the principle of moderation. If a ruler is too strict, severe and does not make himself available, his subordinates will fear him and even distance from him. If a ruler is too friendly, conciliatory and easily available, all types of dissolute proposals and ideas will come forward. Thus, it is important for a wise ruler to keep a balance between being strict and friendly.

In book 18.2, Xunzi believed that rulership/leadership should be earned not inherited. To Xunzi, the worthiest of rulers or leaders will be someone who cultivates **the Way**, carries out his duties morally and does whatever can bring benefit to the people and country. Besides that, a wise ruler also plays the role of teaching and transforming others. In book 18.6, Xunzi advocated that a wise ruler or government should be capable of teaching and transforming both the capable and the incapable. In defining **the Way**, Xunzi in Book 12.8 said,

"If "ritual principles are exalted and the model perfected," then the state had constancy.

If "the worthy are esteemed and the able employed," then the people know the direction

of right conduct.

If "there are continual assessments and impartial evaluations," then the people will not

mistrust the government.

If "effort is rewarded and idleness penalized," then the people will not be indolent.

If "consultations are universal and judgments are uniform," then "the whole world will

come to him as to their home."...." (Knoblock, 1999).

In governing a country, the truly wise ruler protects the arts of civilization so that violent states will become peaceful. In Book 7.5, Xunzi said,

"If the ruler bestows high rank on you and exalts you, be respectful, take strict care to fulfil your duties, and be restrained. If he trusts and loves you, be careful, circumspect, and humble. If he gives you sole authority, hold fast to maintaining your responsibilities and oversee them meticulously. If he is at ease and friendly with you, be cautious of this closeness and do not become corrupt. If the ruler is distant and remote, strive for complete oneness with him but do not oppose him. If he diminishes and degrades you, be fearful and apprehensive but do not harbour resentments..." (Knoblock, 1999).

In Book 14.6, Xunzi divided the effectiveness of a ruler into 3 steps that are:

Step 1: Employ just principles;
Be magnanimous, liberal and forbearing with the people; and
Be respectful and reverent in dealing with people.

Step 2: Apply the principle of 'Mean' (moderation);
Develop social harmony; and
Engage in judicial scrutiny.

Step 3: Promote reward and mete out punishment appropriately and promptly.

A wise ruler needs to carry out all the three steps correctly and thus enjoy long-term political and social order and harmony. The underlying principle that cuts across all the three steps is humaneness. If a man acts in accordance with humane principles, he will certainly become a sage. When abiding with humane principles, a wise man will not boast his virtues and have no reservations about expressing love and respect to others. A wise man always acts and reacts according to the need of the situation – if the situation requires bending, he will do so. Xunzi placed humaneness as top in the priorities of a wise ruler or government. To be humane is to put the interests of people first. In Book 10.17 (Knoblock, 1999), he pointed out that a good government policy should be:

“Benefiting from the people only after first having benefited them > Not benefiting the people yet taking benefits from them”

Benefiting from the people only after first having benefited them	>	**Not benefiting the people yet taking benefits from them**

“Using the people only after having demonstrated love for them > Using the people but not loving them”

Using the people only after having demonstrated love for them	>	**Using the people but not loving them**

A wise government should implement policies on the usage of all resources of a nation to first benefit its people before deriving the benefit itself. Xunzi strongly endorsed using the capable and worthy in the government. In recruitment, a person should be recruited and positioned based on his inner power; his position must then match his salary; and finally his salary should match the services provided. Reward and punishment must be equitable and commensurate with the deeds and wrongdoings respectively. If incentives cannot work, it cannot serve to motive the capable and worthy. If penalties cannot work, the incapable and unworthy will stay. In that case, the capable and worthy will not join the government while the incapable and unworthy will not leave. In defining what determines a strong state or good government, Xunzi said (in Book 10.19),

“If the ruler does not exalt ritual principles, then the army will be weak. If he does not love his people, then the army will be weak. If when he prohibits or approves something he is untrustworthy, then the army will be weak. If his commendations and rewards do not penetrate

down to the lower ranks, then the army will be weak. If the generals and marshals are incapable, then the army will be weak. If the ruler is fond of achievement, then the country will be impoverished. If he is fond of profits, then the country will be poor. If there is multitude of knights and grand officers, then the country will be impoverished. If artisans and merchants are numerous, then the country will be poor. If there is no regulation of the calculations in weighing and measuring, then the country will be poor.

If the lower classes are poor, the ruler will be poor; if they are prosperous, then the ruler will be rich....." (Knoblock, 1999).

Thus, a good government should:

- Highly praise ritual principles;
- Love its people, be trustworthy and use trusted people;
- Have a reward system that diffuses to the lowest level;
- Use capable and worthy people to serve;
- Make both the upper and lower classes prosperous; and
- Regulate the country with proper standards, methods and measurements.

In respect to wealth creation and distribution, Xunzi (in Book 10.2) advocated that upper classes should harvest what is allowable by law while the lower classes should moderate their consumption according to the ritual principles. The upper classes should exploit the lower classes; while the lower classes should live in moderation. The upper classes use their mental power while the lower classes use their physical strength. Both the upper and lower classes should live in prosperity. In governing the different classes in a society, the wise government encourages moderation in the use of resources and goods, lets the people make a generous living and is good at storing up the harvest surplus. In this manner, they will allow the nation to prosper and the multitudes to make a decent and generous living.

In Book 11.17, Xunzi emphasized the elements of laws, scholars (talented or worthy men) and customs (rites, rituals and moral principles) that make a nation strong. He said,

"There is no country that does not possess some laws that are well ordered, and there is no country that does not possess some laws that are anarchic.

There is no country that does not possess some scholars who are worthy, and there is no country that does not have some people who are indolent. There is no country that does not have some people who are respectfully self-restrained, and there is none that does not have some who are violent.

There is no country that does not have some customs that are beautiful and refined, and there is none that does not have some that are ugly and evil... " (Knoblock, 1999).

The above model of governing that combines the humanism principle of Confucius with the legalism principle of Xunzi and Han Fei Zi had been applied by most rulers or emperors in China for over 2,000 years, especially after the Qin Dynasty – that is Humanism with soft Legalism.

In defining the differences between a wise man and a humane man, Xunzi cited Confucius' teaching as follows, from book 29.7 (Knoblock, 1999):

Wise Man	Humane Man
The wise man causes others to know him.	The humane man causes others to love him.
The wise man knows others.	The humane man loves others.
The wise man knows himself.	The humane man loves himself.

The above clearly places the humane man above the wise man. For Xunzi and Confucius, to cause others to know/love oneself is less important than to know/love others. This is why Confucius said, "I do not worry that others do not understand me. I only worry I do not understand others." In addition, to know/love others is more inferior than to know/love oneself.

Xunzi defined the standard behavior of a real gentleman, where he should not be easily carried away by flattery or toadiness. He does not engage in backbiting or slander. However, until today it is still difficult to find someone who possesses these qualities and characteristics of a gentleman. In today's office politics, some of the commonly observed political labels include blaming others, apple polishing, "kissing up", passing the buck, covering the rear, spreading rumors, whistle-blowing, taking advantage of others' weaknesses, claiming credit over others achievements, forming coalitions, creating conflict, scheming over others and being opportunistic/exploitative. But this does not mean that a gentleman does not discriminate. In Book 5.13, Xunzi subscribed to the idea that a gentleman knows when to discriminate between good and bad. To different people, we must use a different treatment or approach. A common saying is, *"Different strokes for different folks."* In addition, Xunzi said,

"Exalted, highly esteemed, and honoured – he does not use these to be arrogant toward others. Astutely intelligent and possessing sage-like wisdom – he does not use these to place others in difficulty. Quick-witted, fluent, agile, and universal in his intellectual grasp – he does not employ these to gain precedence over others. Strong, resolute, brave, and daring – he does not use these to cause injury to others. When he does not know, he asks others; when he lacks an ability, he studies; and even when he possesses an ability, he always yields to others. Only thusly does a man develop inner power……" (Book 6.12, Knoblock, 1999).

In dealing with his subordinates, a gentleman does not use his capability or intelligence to suppress his people or place others in a difficult position. He will always put himself in others' shoes by practicing empathy. Besides that, a gentleman will use his sense of discretion in dealing with his people such as knowing when to speak and knowing when to remain silent, knowing when to trust and knowing when to suspect, and so on. Xunzi said, *"Trusting the trustworthy is trust; suspecting the suspect is also trust. Esteeming the worthy is humaneness; deprecating the unworthy is humaneness as well. Speaking when it is appropriate to do so is knowledge; remaining silent when appropriate is also knowledge. Hence knowing when to remain silent is as important as knowing when to speak. Therefore, a sage, though he speaks often, always observes the logical categories appropriate to what he discusses. .....* (Book 6.11 of Xunzi, Knoblock, 1999). What is most important is when you speak, be genuine and tell the truth.

Xunzi believed a man can transform himself through learning and earnest practice. Upon acquiring inner power, one needs to cultivate uprightness, know one's destiny and manifest what is right and true. Only then can one be called a truly cultivated man. The making of a gentleman focuses on both internal etiquette and external grooming. In contemporary times, basic grooming reflects one's positive image and creates a good impression of oneself. On the other hand, etiquette reflects the rules and regulations for a society to function properly, such as courtesy and consideration. The common saying is, *"Regardless of how you feel inside, always try to look good on the outside."* In Book 5, Xunzi primarily discussed about one's physiognomy (physiognomy involves judging a person's character from the external features).

To physiognomize, the external form is not as important as evaluating one's mind. It is the actions of a man that are more important the mind. If a man's external form appears evil but his mind and actions are good, he will be considered a gentleman. On the other hand, if a man's external appearance looks good (such as being tall, well-built, attractive and handsome) but he possesses an evil mind and performs evil actions, he is far from being a gentleman. As the western saying goes, *"Don't judge a book by its cover."* So, in judging others, do not be deceived by a person's appearance. We need to investigate deeper into his or her thinking and actions. For contemporary times, a "Gentleman Model" has been proposed as per Figure 1.2.

Figure 1.2
The Gentleman Model

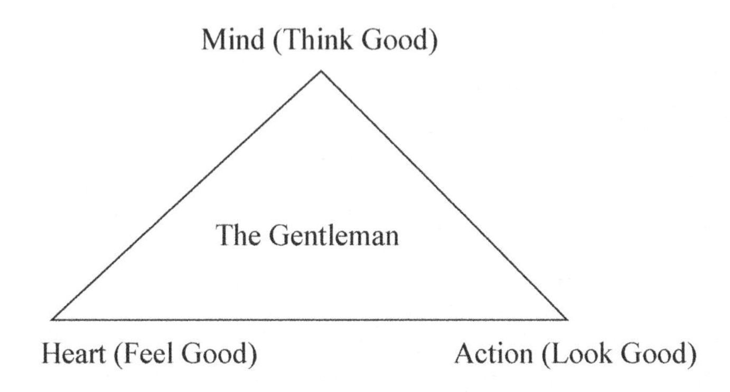

The rationale for the above model is based on the idea that a gentleman begins with the right thinking before that can be translated into good feelings and acting in a positive manner.

Mind (Think Good)

Everything begins from the mind. Part of human civilization or man's evolution is about expanding the mind or intellectual capacity. Besides this, the mind needs to possess the right substance in order to set things right. The mind (in this case referring to the psychological mindset) includes attitude, values and beliefs, perception and personality:

1. Positive Attitude – Always sees the positive side of all events and things. A person with a positive attitude always sees a problem as a challenge or an opportunity, while a person with a negative attitude sees a problem as a threat. A positive attitude translates into good feelings and will add energy to our actions.

2. Right Values and Beliefs – One is able to translate the right values and beliefs, into good habits and through long-term practice, it will shape a person's character and destiny. Habits make a person. We often associate successful or happy people with those possessing many good habits while an unsuccessful or unhappy person's condition is partly due to his/her bad habits.

3. Positive Perception – This is a process by which individuals organize and interpret their sensory impressions in order to give meaning to their environment. People's behavior is based on their perception of what reality is, not on reality itself. The world as it is perceived is the world that is behaviorally important.

4. High Self-Esteem and Confidence – This is belief in self and expectation of success. A person with high self-esteem and confidence often takes more risks and uses unconventional approaches in dealing with things or events.

5. Internal Locus of Control – This is the degree to which people believe they are masters of their own fate. A person with an internal locus of control believes that he/she controls what happens to him/her. This is in contrast to a person with external locus of control who believes that he/she is the victim of the environment and he/she has no choice but to submit to fate or what the Chinese often refer to as "Heaven's Will".

Heart (Feel Good)

Our feelings are expressed in our facial expressions (happy, angry, sad and glad) as well as our verbal and non-verbal language. In interaction with others, the Chinese subscribe to the 'Principle of Reciprocity' – how others treat us depends on how we treat others. Our expression (verbal and non-verbal) is directly and equally related to their response, which is similar to the law of actions:

1. Good Emotional Self-Awareness or Expression - Understand your own emotions and then take control to manage your emotions. Do not allow your emotions to control your mood and your behavior.

2. Good Emotional Awareness of Others - Understand your own environment, and do not adversely become a victim of the environment. Do not allow the environment to control your mood and your behavior. Be sensitive and confident when interacting with others. Develop a positive personality and expressions. Be affirmative and not aggressive.

Action (Look Good)

The Chinese philosophers strongly emphasize on one's behavior or action. To the Chinese, it is so much easier to say something than to reflect it in our actions. In presenting oneself, the Chinese pay attention to external appearance and internal quality:

1. Right personality- In Western study, man's personality can be grouped into different categories that make people different. Personality can be defined as the way we carry ourselves in front of others. A person with outgoing personality would be able to project more friendly and supportive behavior.

2. Open and effective communication

    - Learn to speak and write well. Use the language of contemporary times that directly links to our day-to-day living.

    - If you have nothing nice to say, don't say anything. Don't complaint behind others' backs.

    - Know how to compliment and be polite. Be sincere in what you say. Say what you mean and mean what you say.

- Know how to say something well and understand the power of words. Speak what you want to say and express it in the manner you want it to be transmitted.
- Be a good listener, and listen until you understand. If you do not understand, ask for clarity.
- Speak with sense. Do not speak nonsense – avoid speaking so profoundly that others are unable to use their senses to perceive your words. In speaking, simplify complex matters in a way that is simple and easily understood.

3. Right Body Language

- Facial expressions are used in expressing happiness, anger, sadness and gladness. Use the right facial expressions to express your inner state. Do not fake it.
- The tone of our voice and inflection (emphasis) is important. Use a soft tone when putting across your opinions or points. Avoid using a tone that can be interpreted as arrogant.
- Body language should be appropriate. Avoid looking arrogant or all-knowing. Use body language to reinforce the verbal communication. It must be consistent.
- Physical distance depends on the level of intimacy to the person.

4. Basic Grooming, Etiquette and Encouraging Behavior

- Have good manners - Be courteous and respectful.
- Show sensitivity and compassion to others.
- Be trustworthy, humble and considerate.
- Project yourself in a positive manner.
- Be cheerful.

It is important for us to understand that how we think directly influences how we feel and it will ultimately influence how we act. Negative thinking will lead to negative emotion and behavior. On the other hand, positive thinking will lead to positive emotions and behavior. It is essential to develop a positive mindset (thinking) as positive thinking will **"add energy"** to your actions while negative thinking will **"subtract/minus energy"** from your actions. In interpersonal relationships,

"Be simple and genuine, more real."
"If we learn to forgive others, others will ignore our mistakes, too."

In distinguishing a gracious society from an ugly society, Xunzi subscribed to the use of a developmental model (through education, ritual and moral principles) as well as the use of a control model (through strict and harsh punishment, rules and regulations) to cultivate a gracious society. To Xunzi, without installing a proper legal system with a penal code, the aim of cultivating a gracious society is almost impossible.

Refinement through Learning

To Xunzi, the qualities of a gentleman are not inborn, and they are acquired through constant cultivation and earnest practice. This explains the importance of having the right ritual and moral principles to guide and circumscribe human beliefs and behaviors. As these are learned behaviors (nurture rather than nature), Xunzi strongly emphasized the purpose of learning and the role of a teacher in transmitting these values. In defining the meaning of learning, Xunzi discussed much about man's inborn nature, the concept of conscious exertion, the meaning of names and words, and the purpose of learning in Book 19 to 22,. In defining the development of a man, Xunzi subscribed to the idea that the making of a man is divided as:

Inborn nature + Conscious Activity/Exertion
= Development of a Man

To Xunzi, man from birth possesses an awareness and memory in retaining what he has learned from the environment. It is through conscious activity and exertion that man is able to gain a perception of things. Without the ability to remember, there is nothing for conscious activity to change or improve. If there is no conscious activity to exert, there will be no improvement and refinement to transform and transmute the individual. Learning is the process of purifying the mind. When the inner mind becomes pure, ritual will be observed and conduct will be perfected.

It is a common flaw of man to be blinded to some points of the truth and thus, shut his mind to the principles of righteousness. In Book 21.5, Xunzi discussed about man being blinded by utility, desires, law and technique. If a man is blinded by utility, he will only pursue profit. If a man is blinded by his own desires, he will only concentrate on satisfaction. If a man is blinded by law, he will only focus on logic and enforcement. If a man is blinded by technique or method, he will not pursue knowledge. Once a man is blinded by these flaws, it will bring disorder and misfortune to himself and others. In a family, it will bring disharmony among family members. In an organization, the morale of the employees will be low. In a society, it will bring social disorder and unrest. That is why, being moral, wise and humane are the fundamentals of a man. If a man is upright, honest advice will come forward while slanderous words will be turned away. He will attract gentlemen while petty men will keep a distance. A gentleman who is enlightened will transform his followers.

The faculty of knowing belongs to the inborn nature of man. Man uses his innate faculty to understand the operations of Nature that allow things to be known. Through the wrong, one is able to see the right and through the right, one is able to see the wrong. In Book 22.1 of Xunzi, he further described the inborn nature of emotions as the feelings of like and dislike, delight and anger, and sorrow and joy. The ability to choose the different emotions is called "thinking". It is the thinking ability of man that allows one to acquire external things into their thinking process which is called "conscious exertion". Through continuous learning and refinement, man can develop his capacity of knowing to a level called "awareness" (Knoblock, 1999).

Xunzi devoted Book 22 entirely to elaborating on the meaning of things. To Xunzi, a wise man is able to make distinctions and separations among different things. Through our five sense organs – eye, ear, mouth, nose and body – the mind is able to differentiate between pleasure and anger, sorrow and joy, and love and hate. In this manner, it heightens our awareness of things at the cognitive level. Once the mind is able to differentiate different things, a name is given. The myriad of things in Nature will be studied and investigated by man and subsequently classified as different things with different names.

Although these myriad things share the same world, they have different forms with different features and characteristics. Similarly, by nature all human beings are the same, but due to different upbringing, they have different degrees of awareness and use different methods to pursue their desires. In the world, all things are divided or classified into different orders of things such humans, animals, birds, insects, etc. For example, if a group of living things is called "bird", they will all share certain common characteristics as creatures with two legs, two wings and able to fly. A tiger can be defined as a large, fierce animal of the cat family, yellow-skinned with black stripes. Similar the meaning of "insect" can be defined as a type of small animal normally having six legs, with no backbone and a body divided into three parts that are the head, thorax and abdomen. However, over time, all things go through transformation in their appearance, functions or features. Over a longer period of evolution, a new name may be given.

When man uses different names to describe or differentiate things, it is done in order to explain and justify his actions. It is generally considered wrong to kill a 'man' but not to kill a 'murderer'. By giving a thing a different name (from a 'man' to a 'murderer'), it can justify one's action of executing him. Besides this, names are used to define different realities to express ideas. Name should clearly and fully convey the meaning that they define. When a correct name is used to convey meaning, everything will conform to the "Way" and order will be ensured with a clear intention. A wise man uses the right names and words to express his intentions while a petty man uses his words to deceive others. The speech of a gentleman is easy to understand, to establish and to act upon.

In Book 22.11, Xunzi put forward the concept that man is born with natural desires but it is the mind that acts to control and moderate it. If a man's desires are excessive, his actions will exceed his abilities and thus, it will bring misery to himself. If one's desires cannot be fully met by one's abilities, he or she should choose to moderate his pursuit. It is alright for one to have desires for a better life, but it must be realistic. If **a person's desires exceed his or her abilities**, dissatisfaction and misery will follow. On the other hand, if **a person's abilities exceed his or her desires**, satisfaction and happiness will follow. If a person's desires exceed his abilities, he or she could either moderate the desires downward or take steps to gradually improve his or her abilities. If he or she pursues the desires, he or she may resort to unscrupulous means to satisfy the desires. Thus, the importance of learning is emphasized. To Xunzi, learning set people apart. In Book 1.9, Xunzi said,

"The learning of the gentleman enters through the ear, is stored in the mind, spreads through the four limbs, and is visible in his activity and repose. In his softest word and slightest movement, in one and all, the gentleman can be taken as a model and pattern. The learning of the petty man enters the ear and comes out the mouth. Since the distance between the mouth and ear is no more than four inches, how could it be sufficient to refine the seven-foot of a man!" (Knoblock, 1999).

To be able to put into practice what one has learnt is the ultimate purpose of learning. As described by Xunzi, a gentleman is able to practice what he has learnt while an inferior/petty man can only echo what he has learnt. In contemporary times and in terms of learning, man can be categorized into 3 types with respect to this:

- The learning of the **inferior man** enters through one ear and exits through another ear.
- The learning of the **average man** enters through one ear and comes out through the mouth.
- The learning of the **superior man** enters through one ear, is assimilated and internalized into the mind and translated into actions or behaviors. It is through long-term practice that it will become the habit of a person.

The key purpose of learning is to improve oneself and in the long run transform oneself from an ordinary person into a wise person or a Sage. *"In antiquity men undertook learning for the sake of self-improvement; today people undertake learning for the sake of others. The learning of the gentleman is used to refine his character...."* (Book 1.10, Knoblock, 1999). Most of man's behavior is learnt or acquired behavior rather than innate or inborn behavior. It is through earnest and long-term practice that these behaviors are internalized and become the good habits of a man (habits can be defined as the second-nature of man). There are many books that have been written on the good habits that make an effective, successful or happy person. The average Chinese believes that:

"Values shape a person's behavior which in turn develops into a person's habits and build a person's character, and which will ultimately determine a person's destiny."

In respect of learning and action, Xunzi said,

""I once spent a whole day in thought, but it was not so valuable as a moment in study. I once stood on my tiptoes to look out into the distance, but it was not so effective as climbing up to a high place for a broader vista...... A man who borrows a horse and carriage does not improve his feet, but he can extend his travels 1,000 li. A man who borrows a boat and paddles does not gain any new ability in water, but he can cut across rivers and seas. The gentleman

by birth is not different other men; he is just good at 'borrowing' the use of external things." (Book 1.3 – Knoblock, 1999)

Xunzi's thoughts about learning are consistent with Confucius who emphasized on "do first and talk later". To a large extent, the Chinese subscribe to action learning. In Book 2.9, Xunzi said, *"Though the Way is near, if you do not travel along it, you will not reach the end. Though the task is small, if it is not acted upon, it will not be completed. One who spends many days in idleness will not excel others by much."* (Knoblock, 1999). He subscribed to 'learning is to gain knowledge and it is through earnest practice that one can master it'. As the saying goes, **"If you teach a person a concept, he will remember for a week. If you show a person how the concept works, he will remember for a month. If you let the person do it himself, he will remember over his lifetime."** This is the Chinese definition of 'being practical or pragmatic' – practice makes perfect. To the average Chinese,

- ☐ "A person who talks but does not act is called a **petty/ inferior man**"
- ☐ "A person who talks and keep to his promise is called a **gentleman**"
- ☐ "A person who acts first and talks later is called a **sage**"
- ☐ "A person who acts but does not claim credit is called a **selflessness man**"

Xunzi believed that it is through learning that one's perspective can be broadened. To Xunzi, learning is an on-going process and it is not an end. In explaining what is learning, Xunzi wrote in Book 1.1, *"The gentleman says: 'Learning must never be concluded.' Though blue dye comes from the indigo plant, it is bluer than indigo. Ice is made from water, but it is colder than water……"* (Knoblock, 1999) Learning does not exist in isolation. There is always a synergistic effect. When new learning interacts with our past learning and knowledge, it will create a total larger than the sum of the individual parts. Besides this, Xunzi subscribed to learning through engaging more of our senses – such as seeing, hearing and feeling. In Book 1.2, Xunzi said, *"Truly if you do not climb a high mountain, you will be unaware of the height of the sky. If you do not look down into a deep gorge, you will be unaware of the thickness of the earth. If you have not heard the words inherited from the Ancient Kings, you will be unaware of the greatness of learning and inquiry..... There is no spirit so great as the transformation of the self with the Way, and there is no blessing so long-lasting as being without misfortune."* (Knoblock, 1999) It is through the search and **re**-search (search again) for knowledge coupled with deep inquiry and reflection that one's perspective on things can be **deepened, broadened and heightened**.

The real purpose of learning is to first create a scholar and finally to develop a Sage. Like Confucius, Xunzi emphasized that in learning, one needs to genuinely accumulate and earnestly practice over a long period to see the results. In Book 1.8, Xunzi emphasized that one should not be tired of learning and it should be continued until death. This analogy is similar to today's concept of life-long learning, especially in the information age or knowledge society. Learning and continuous practice to master it is the best way to keep us relevant and useful to society. To be able to see the result of one's own learning, one must exercise perseverance. In Book 1.6, Xunzi said, "…… *If you accumulate enough good to make whole your inner power, a divine clarity of intelligence will be naturally acquired and a sage-like mind will be fully realised……*" (Knoblock, 1999) Learning will be able to help us to gain knowledge but it is through practice that we can master it. In order for one to master any subject matter, continuous and earnest practice is the only way. That's why we normally say:

"Practice makes perfect"
- to master a skill or technique, it is through practice, practice and more practice.

Ranked Hierarchy

To Xunzi, in order for the entire population to live in harmony and unity, they need to be circumscribed by regulations, rituals and moral principles with ranked hierarchy or social classes or structure. In his Book 4.14, Xunzi described social classes in terms of:

- Different status between the upper position and the lower position.
- Different privileges of the old and the youth.
- Division between the wise and the stupid, the capable and the incapable.

If a society exists without different classes, there will be no proper arrangement of society where authority will be evenly distributed and thus, there will be no unity and capable people will not be willing to serve. With social classes or structures, all men will have to perform their duties accordingly and the remuneration will be based on their positions and roles. In Chinese society, the average Chinese places great emphasis on the hierarchy and his or her position in the hierarchy in determining how they behave and carry themselves. Each and every one has a position in the social hierarchy with defined standard roles, responsibilities and behaviors. The respect and compliance of the social hierarchy and structure directly contributes to social stability and harmony within Chinese society. From a young age, the compliance of the Chinese child to the family hierarchy is highly praised as "obedience" which is the highest form of good within the Chinese family. When the child matures, social compliance and respect of hierarchy become social norms that are highly praised.

In Book 10.1, Xunzi further reiterated that if different classes and divisions did not exist in a society, the proper relationship between superior and subordinates would never be established. Thus, it would be difficult for a superior to regulate his subordinates. It is essential for a society to have different divisions and classes that are clearly defined in order for that society to function properly and in an orderly way. In addition to the establishment of a hierarchical structure and system, the role and responsibility for each position need to be clearly defined and well-circumscribed by ritual principles or else disorder will result. If the ritual principles are not well-followed where the young insult the old and the strong bully the weak, then the old and the weak will suffer.

The description of a ranked hierarchy is similar to organizational structure and design practice in a contemporary organization where works are categorized based on work specialization with well-defined reporting relationships. Based on the organizational structure, a comprehensive and equitable reward system will be developed. In the Chinese organization, the average Chinese employee is expected to respect and behave in conformity to the organizational hierarchy and authority. It is a taboo for one to question the authority of those at the top of the hierarchy. This is still commonly observed in today's organizational behavior in many Chinese-owned and Chinese-managed enterprises. In Book 11.20, Xunzi said,

"In a well-ordered country, where class distinctions have been fixed, from the ruler to the prime minister to the ministers down to the most minor officials, each person will pay attention only to his official duties and will not strive to adjudicate what is not part of his duties. Each person will pay attention to only to what is within the purview of his office and will not strive to oversee what lies outside it...." In Book 11.18, Xunzi further reiterated that, *"Lord and minister, superior and inferior, noble and base, old and young, down to commoners – all should exalt this as the standard of rectitude. Only in this way will all examine themselves to ensure that they devote their attention to the tasks of their social class..."* (Knoblock, 1999).

In many of Xunzi's works, much was discussed about the importance of ranked hierarchy and its related functions, practices and issues. He often relates a person's functions, roles and responsibilities with his position. In the government, the sage King should first exercise his responsibilities and duties as the highest in the hierarchy while the lower officers should not neglect their duties in execution. In this manner, the commoners would live in harmony and would not commit offences of theft and banditry. The government should lead its people to the right path by letting them clearly perceive that it is impossible for theft and robbery to lead to riches. For this reason, moral sanctions and punishments would be extremely rare. These things were recorded in Book 24.2 of Xunzi. In Book 16.2, Xunzi categorized awe-inspiring authority into three varieties:

- that instilled by the influence of the Way and its Power;
- that instilled by harsh and cruel judicial investigations; and
- that instilled by deranged madness.

Xunzi was in favour of awe-inspiring authority that is instilled by the influence of the Way and its Power. In defining what is the Way, Xunzi (Book 16.4) described the Way as ritual and moral principles, polite refusals and deference to others, and loyalty and trustworthiness. With respect to establishing the line of authority within the hierarchy, Xunzi made a distinction between 'to possess the way of domination' and 'to win a position of power that permits one to dominate others'. He was definitely in favor of the former than the latter. The position of a ruler or that of a prime minister was about being bestowed with a position that gave one the power to dominate. The position of a ruler is the highest in the hierarchy likened to the Chief Executive Officer (CEO) of a business organization. On the other hand, the position of a prime minister is such where he can dominate everybody below him but is only accountable to a ruler is likened to the General Manager (GM) of a business organization. In executing one's position of power, Xunzi (in Book 16.4) emphasized that power has to be circumscribed by moral principles and should act in the interests of the multitude (the public). He further reiterated that a person with power should:

- treat right as right, wrong as wrong, the capable as capable, and the incapable as incapable; and

- power has to be circumscribed by 'justice and morality' and it should be applied to all people; among lord and subject, superior and subordinate, old and young, even down to the lowest commoner.

A cultivated man is devoted to cultivating his inner self – to unify rules and regulations, exalt ritual and moral principles. In contrast, the uncultivated man is just the opposite – forming cliques and building relationships to enhance his position. An intelligent ruler understands this and in assigning high official positions, he will first examine the inner power of the candidates. In execution, especially enforcing power to the extreme, the importance of justice and morality should be embraced. Otherwise there will be a tendency to abuse the power given. If the above is not properly carried out, the government will be in a chaotic situation where it will give birth to deceitful ministers and avaricious officers to the extent that commoners will be greedy, like to spread false rumors and be boastful. In Chinese history, there are many examples of Sage Kings as well as Bad Rulers. As a wise ruler, it is important to note that the people place high importance on life and on living peacefully. If a country is governed through proper rites, rituals and moral principles, nurturing life and the enjoyment of peace will be a natural outcome.

In contemporary times, an organizational leader needs to ensure an organization hierarchy is created, to put the right person to do the right job, to support the building of relationships among employees and ultimately, bring the best out of its people to the highest level. An organization structure should not be seen as a 'power structure' which people use to satisfy personal power needs or use the power given to take advantage of others for personal gain. In defining authority in the hierarchy, an organization needs to abide by the following which are in line with Xunzi's thoughts:

- the position or rank must commensurate the authority and power;

- the position or rank must commensurate the capability; and
- the position or rank must commensurate the moral worth.

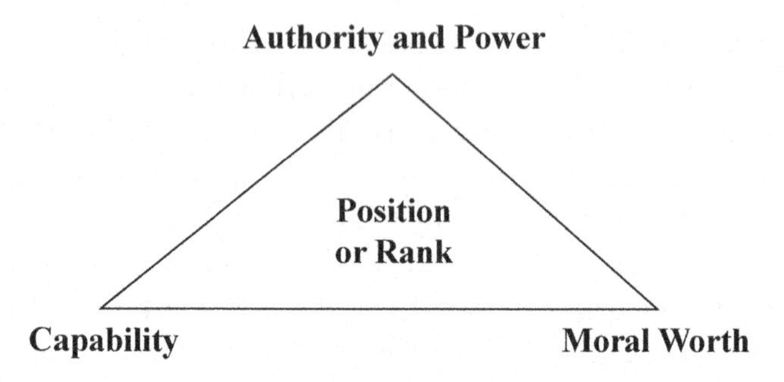

In considering authority and power as well as capability and moral worth, it should be moral worth that comes first. Once the moral worth of a person has been determined and established, then we may seek for someone with capability. If both the morality and capability have been determined, it is then appropriate to delegate the right amount of authority and power in line with the position or rank awarded. When holding a position of great importance, a person must be endowed with high responsibility and authority and be wise in execution. In Book 7.6, Xunzi proposed that when one is in a high position, he must abide by the following four elements:

- be friendly and cooperative with colleagues;
- be supportive of the worthy;
- be kind to all by putting away old grudges if any; and
- do nothing that will block or harm others.

When one's ability is equal to his responsibility, he or she can pay full attention to the execution. When one's ability is insufficient to bear responsibility, it is even more important to abide with the above four elements. In this way, one will avoid disastrous consequences. In allocating a new position, one needs to consider the person's ability, as well as the responsibility and authority attached to the position. There must be a balance between ability, responsibility and authority.

Penal Laws and Punishments

During the warring states era, much of the intellectual debates were focused on the issue of good government which should be based on having good people or having effective laws. Confucians place the virtues of humaneness and the development of the moral character above all other considerations. Confucius was not in favour of using punishment. Confucius said:

"If we lead people by laws and then regulate them with penalties, there will be no sense of shame,

If you lead people by virtue and then circumscribe them with proper rules of conduct, they will develop a sense of shame and hence become good citizens."

- The Analects (2,3) by Khu, *et al.*, 1991

Both Confucius and Mencius subscribed to the notion that Man is by nature kind and good. The Confucians maintained that people should be governed by proper rules of conduct and morality. Based on the assumption that human nature is good, one would be able to cultivate a person's character and train one's personality through proper education both at home and in school. The Master believed that a person needs to cultivate himself from young or else he will have nothing to narrate to others when he has matured.

It is not necessary to punish a person who breaks the law just to remind the law-abiding people. The actions of a person, Confucius believed, are the product of his heart's desire. Confucius was very good at gently leading a man to the path of virtues or persuading him to observe those codes of conduct that are becoming of a cultured person. In the words of Confucius:

"It is not necessary to punish the lawless (the person who breaks the laws) just to remind the law abider. If a gentleman desires to be good, he will naturally be good. Let us assume the virtue of the gentleman is the wind and the people are the weeds. When the wind blows, the weeds will have no choice but to bend."

- The Analects (12,19) by Khu, *et al*., 1991

On the other hand, the legalists believed that a country blessed with good men is no guarantee that it will be governed well. Thus, having an effective legal system is a pre-requisite. In respect of this, Mencius took a middle path where good government is a combination of the right kind of men and the right kind of laws. To Xunzi who strongly advocated the evil nature of man, the emphasis should be on reforming the evil nature of man first before circumscribing them with strict laws and harsh punishment. In maintaining an orderly and harmonious society, Xunzi subscribed to the development of penal laws and punishments. To Xunzi, the punishment must first fit the crime. If the punishments exceeded the crimes, or the crimes exceeded the punishments, the laws would lose their effectiveness. The penal sanctions set the boundary and all people should behave within the boundary or else he or she would be punished.

In Book 24.4, Xunzi proposed a member of the family to be used in judging the offence and the genealogy (the past descent of a family) to be used to recommend the worthy. For this reason, if a man committed an offence, three full generations would be destroyed. This is particularly so in the Chinese mindset where filial piety was extended to the ancestor (near and distant ancestors) in determining the value and worth of a person. In Book 24.3, Xunzi further proposed that in meting out punishment, it has to be impartial. If a father was executed, his son could still serve the government. Similarly, if the elder brother was killed, the younger brother could still be employed. For centuries, the average Chinese family has believed that in bringing up their children, strict discipline and punishment are unavoidable. It is not uncommon that most Chinese parents keep a cane at home for disciplining their children. At least, the cane can be used as a 'deterrent' for any form of defiant behaviors. At schools, it is commonly observed that Chinese school teachers use a cane to discipline naughty young students. At the national level, many Chinese societies still practice 'caning' as part of the punishment for certain crimes.

In meting out punishment, a good ruler/government should be strict and impartial. If a ruler honors those who are greedy and uncivilized instead of punishing them, he actually sends the wrong message to the people. On the other hand, if a ruler metes out punishment impartially, good moral conduct will prevail and evil will be eliminated. Similarly, if a ruler dismisses a good man, then all good men will lose heart and leave office. In book 28.3, Xunzi further emphasized that punishments should be just and the executions have to be just, too. If a country is well-governed, the ruler will let the majestic authority be stern and fierce, but need not wield it. The punishments will be established, but need not be used. If a country is not properly governed, punishments may be frequent but evil is not overcome (Knoblock, 1999).

In Asian society, the use of collective rewards and collective punishments has proven to be effective. Many empirical studies for Asian societies reveal a high level of **Collectivism** (a lower level of Individualism) as compared to Western societies (such as the average American and European who are normally known to be individualistic). A higher level of Collectivism can be interpreted as:

- People born into extended families or other in-groups that continue to protect them in exchange for loyalty.
- From a young age, one has become used to learning to think in terms of "we". Identity is based in the social network to which one belongs.
- Group orientation is emphasized higher than individual interest. Harmony should always be maintained and direct confrontations avoided.

- Trespassing leads to shame and loss of face for self and group.
- Employer-employee relationships are perceived in moral terms, like a family link.
- Relationships prevail over tasks, especially group relationships and harmony.

In designing an effective reward and punishment system, both the individual and the group should be properly emphasized. For example, during the Asian currency crisis in 1997/8 and the Global Financial crisis in 2008/9, many Asian companies embarked on pay cuts instead of retrenchment in order to protect the jobs of their employees. In doing this, an overall pay cut would mean everybody in the organization 'suffers' collectively whereas with retrenchment, only a smaller percentage of the staff would suffer. This is the spirit of collective punishment. On the other hand, during good times, rewards should be shared among groups at the department and division levels as well as at the organizational level. It has been observed that many Asian companies do not highly reward individuals nor overly-punish them. This is because, to the Asians, success or failure is the collective effort of everybody, as all individuals, sections, divisions and departments are part of the organization. Team spirit instead of the 'individual hero' would be highly praised. Employees work best when they feel they belong to a team. This is especially true in a highly collective society. Increasing team work and team spirit within and among different departments in an organization will also proportionally reduce office politics. In leading an Asian company, creating a 'super-team' instead of an 'individual hero' would be part and parcel of good management practice.

In book 18.3, Xunzi said the purpose of punishments is to maintain good social order. The fundamental reason for punishment is to prohibit acts of violence as well as to deter others from committing them in the future. In meting out punishment, overly punitive measures or under-punishing can be equally bad. Punishment must be balanced against the offence or else there will be chaos. Heavy or light punishment varies from time to time and situation to situation. During orderly times, punishment has to be harsh, while during chaotic times, punishment has to be lighter. There must be a balance between "reward" and "punishment". An effective reward and punishment system should be designed in a manner where it will handsomely reward the top 20% of performers (top performers) while at the same time deal with the lowest 20% of performers (poor performers) through punishment (such as demotion, layoff/termination, decrease in salary, no bonus). In many Asian organizations, it is far easier to reward people than to punish. However, an effective performance management system should put equal emphasis on both reward and punishment. If the capable are rewarded while the incapable are not appropriately punished or discouraged, the capable will leave. This kind of reward and punishment system is rather difficult to implement in the Asian context as Asian companies, in general, are more relationship-oriented than task or performance-oriented. It has been observed in many Asian organizations that discharging employees on the grounds of poor performance is uncommon. However, this scenario is gradually changing with time.

The Reward and Punishment System

The relationship between a leader and his followers is closely inter-dependent and related. A leader is likened to a 'ship' while the followers are the 'water'. 'Water' can support a ship to float higher, but on the other hand, 'water' can also capsize a ship and turn it upside down. If a leader treats his followers well, his followers will support him and help them all in achieving a higher level of excellence. Bad or inappropriate leadership may spell disaster. As the tradition says:

"The lord is the boat; his subjects the water. It is the water that sustains the boat,
and it is the water that capsizes the boat."

(Book 9.4 of Xunzi, Knoblock, 1999).

If a leader acts correctly, the followers will respond accordingly. Similarly if a leader acts incorrectly, the followers will also respond accordingly. If a leader does not act, the followers will have nothing to respond to. The action of the followers is the mirror-image of the leader's. In this case, the leader and the followers will have no means of relying upon each other. In such a situation, it would be equivalent to not having a leader. In book 18.1 of Xunzi, he wrote:

"........ *If the superior exhibits and elucidates the standard, his subordinates will be orderly and manageable. If the superior is correct and sincere, his subordinates will be attentive and diligent. If the superior is impartial and right, his subordinates will be amenable and honest. If they are orderly and manageable, they are easily unified. If they are attentive and diligent, they are easily employed. If they are amenable and honest, they are easily understood. When the people are easily unified, there is strength; when they are easily employed, there is accomplishment; when they are easily understood, there is an atmosphere of openness and forthrightness – and this is what produces order.*

If the superior is secretive and mysterious, his subordinates will be suspicious and confused. If he is obscure and inaccessible, his subordinates will be furtive and treacherous. If the superior is biased and one-sided, his subordinates will form parties and cliques. If they are suspicious and confused, they are difficult to unify. If they are furtive and treacherous, they are difficult to employ. If they form parties and cliques, they are difficult to know. When the people are difficult to unify, there is no strength; when they are difficult to employ, there is no accomplishment; and when they are difficult to know, there is no atmosphere of openness and forthrightness – and this is what creates chaos........... " (Knoblock, 1999).

With respect to talent management, Xunzi placed great emphasis on installing an effective structure with a comprehensive reward and punishment system to support human resource development. From antiquity to today, the good principles of ranked hierarchy and structuring are always relevant and important for one to follow. To Xunzi (in Book 24.5), if the above principles are closely followed, people will understand what is valuable and what is beneficial. Not only will the responsibilities and duties be properly discharged, but the real worth of a person will be realized. If we use a person's strengths wisely, we will **manage** him like a **talent**. That is **talent management** in today's context. Employing the right person and placing them in the right job is part and parcel of talent management. Everybody was created with their usefulness. Nobody is created useless. Everybody can be managed like a 'talent'. A wise leader or ruler listens broadly and examines thoroughly into things with intelligence in determining what is right and what is wrong. Only then will he **reward and punish promptly** and appropriately. A wise ruler will make his nation comfortable enough for the people to stay and to attract talented people to come. As Xunzi said in Book 14.2,

"When the streams and ponds are deep, fish and turtles are attracted to make their home in them. When mountain forests flourish, animals and birds are attracted to make their homes there. Where the government and punishments are equitable, the Hundred Clans are attracted to make their homes there. Where ritual and moral principles are perfected, the gentleman will be attracted to make his home there..." (Knoblock, 1999).

The above passage from Xunzi clearly demonstrates the importance of circumscribing a country with ritual and moral principles before capable and worthy people will be attracted. Similarly, an organization is a place where many young scholars choose to excel and give their best. Thus, an organizational leader should instill a good corporate culture that supports effective performance with a conducive working environment before capable people will be attracted. At the end of the day, man needs to be motivated using incentives in order to sustain his enthusiasm. As the saying goes, if you want a monkey to climb enthusiastically, you need to give the monkey a tree tall enough to climb. Similarly if you want your employees to work enthusiastically, you need to provide a hierarchy high enough for the employees to climb, supported by a comprehensive incentive and reward system.

The key difference between effective and ineffective leaders lies in their ability to attract, retain and motivate capable people to work for them. In explaining the difference between an intelligent ruler and a benighted ruler, Xunzi highlighted the following:

- The intelligent ruler honors the worthy and employs the able while the benighted ruler is jealous of the worthy, fears the able and would hide their accomplishments.

- The intelligent ruler rewards loyalty while the benighted ruler does the opposite. If a man condemns the worthy, he is himself unworthy.

If a ruler is fond of avaricious profits, then his ministers, down to the lowest level will take advantage of their positions for personal gain. If a ruler is fond of rituals and moral principles with no mind for avaricious profits, his subjects will show deference, be loyal and trustworthy and will give their best in the administration of the state. In the organizational context, a wise leader is generous enough to share his profits with his employees. When his organizational makes profits, he will first thank his employees before his management team and himself.

A wise ruler or leader should be wise in recruiting and selecting his right- and left-hand people to form a strong team. The success of a country or an organization is a team effort. Without having a strong team, success will be difficult. Thus, a wise ruler or leader needs to employ the right people to be in his team of ministers. In selecting the right ministers, Xunzi categorized ministers into four different types (in Book 13.1) as follows:

> *"Accordingly, one who employs Sage ministers will become a King;*
> *one who employs meritorious ministers will be strong;*

one who employs presumptuous ministers will be endangered; and
one who employs sham ministers will be doomed..." (Knoblock, 1999)

A minister who puts the interest of his or her ruler first regardless of the ruler's mandate is seen to have loyalty. A loyal minister is not the same as an "obedient" one – a form of blind loyalty. A loyal minister may or may not follow the mandate of his ruler but he will always put the interest of the ruler first. If a ruler uses upright and just people to be his ministers, the nation will progress. If a ruler uses remonstrating and wrangling ministers, the nation will move backward. In serving a Sage ruler, ministers only need to follow orders and carry them through. In serving a mediocre ruler, ministers need to engage in discussions and arguments instead of merely following orders. The relationship between a ruler and his ministers is inter-twined and mutually inter-dependent. In China, the downfall of many dynasties was partly due to the rulers employing the wrong ministers. Similarly, the CEO of an organization has to be careful and wise in selecting his right- and left-hand people or-else disaster will follow. The success of a ruler is not confined to just attracting the worthy but rather, in being sincere and rigorous enough in using the worthy. In treating worthy and unworthy people, different approaches should be applied:

- With a worthy person, one should honor, respect and try to stay close to him or her.
- With an unworthy person, one should be cautious, fearful and keep a distance but still show respect to him or her.

For Xunzi (in Book 13.9), showing respect is the basic ritual for all interpersonal relationships. Whether it is treating a worthy or unworthy man, one should demonstrate a high degree of "humaneness" that includes loyalty, trustworthiness, straightforwardness, diligence and not cause harm to others. In the recruitment and selection exercise, by employing the right person of the right capabilities and moral worth and placing them in a ranked hierarchy, the King will be honored and the subjects will be contented. In contemporary times, this practice is always relevant. In recruitment, if an organization brings in capable people, the less-capable ones will leave. On the other hand, if an organization begins to recruit less-capable people, the existing capable employees will either perish or leave and that is the beginning of a disaster. Similarly, an organization should be very careful in recruitment and selection of new employees so that the existing capable employees can be retained. Thus, the new and existing employees need to be treated fairly in respect to reward and punishment. In Book 16.3, Xunzi said, "……… *Indeed 'to honour the worthy and employ the able' and 'to reward where there is achievement and punish where there is fault' are not the idiosyncracies of a single individual….*" (Knoblock, 1999).

The wise ruler knows how to honor capable people with rank and attractive remuneration. When a ruler gains something, he does not keep everything for himself. You must learn to share credit with your people. Rewards and punishments have to be clear. Although they are on opposite sides of the coin, they are inseparable. This strategy is commonly used among large corporations to compete for the best brains to work for them. If a ruler does nothing to use the capable and does not dismiss the incapable, the capable would go into seclusion and not serve the country. On the contrary, the incapable would hold high positions. If an organization leader uses a talented employee like a slave, good people will leave the organization, thus he or she will be unable to retain good people within the organization. To be able to retain good people within the organization is the most important factor in sustaining the competitiveness of a business. In the organizational context, while it is important to reward top or star performers, it is also important that we do not condone poor performers and those with bad conduct. At times, it is important to punish one as an example to warn the multitudes. The principle of using rewards and punishments towards capable and incapable people has to be properly implemented to ensure equity and justice. The capable one has to be handsomely rewarded as an important reinforcement. In antiquity, enlightened rulers set up great tasks to be accomplished and established great rewards to achieve great achievements. Similarly, in contemporary times, wise organizational leaders should develop and implement effective performance management systems that will not only support the employees to achieve new milestones but to bring the best out of them. To the legalist, the influence of a ruler or leader is based on the use of appropriate rewards and punishments as a device for managing and directing the ministers, as Xunzi pointed out in Book 14.10 that:

- In rewarding, one should not confer more than is warranted or else the benefits may extend to the petty man.

- In punishing, one should not go to wrongful excess or else the injury may reach the gentleman.

CHAPTER 2
HAN FEI ZI

Han Fei Zi (韓非子), born around 280 B.C., was a prince of the Han State as well as a scholar of Chinese political science of the Warring States Era. He crystallised his thoughts in some 55 essays or sections. Han Fei Zi believed man to be naturally evil, for whom strict rules and severe punishments are needed. His writings came into the hands of the King of Qin (also known as Shi Huang Di) who subsequently conquered and ruled all China under the title of the First Emperor of China. However, before Han Fei Zi manages to meet up the King of Qin, his former fellow classmate, Li Si intervened and warned the King that Han Fei Zi was a royal member of the Han State and that his royalty might be doubtful (Watson, 1964). Instead of meet up with Han Fei Zi, the King of Qin sent him to prison for investigation. Subsequently, Li Si sent poison to the prison which Han Fei Zi drank it. He died in 233 B.C. (Tsai, 1991-b and Watson, 1964). Han Fei Zi subscribed to the Legalist school of thought. Although he is not the inventor of legalism in China, he has however made major contribution in perfecting it.

Han Fei Zi fully subscribed to 'rule by law' instead of 'rule by virtue'. To Han Fei Zi,

"When a sage rules a state, he does not depend on people's doing good of themselves; he sees to it that they are not allowed to do what is bad. If he depends on people's doing good of themselves, then within his borders he can count on less than ten instances of success. But

if he sees to it that they are not allowed to do what is bad, then the whole state can be brought to a uniform level of order. Those who rule must employ measures that will be effective with the majority and discard those that will be effective with only a few. Therefore they devote themselves not to virtue but to law." (quoted from "The Great Thoughts of China" by Liang Congjie, page133).

Han Fei Zi's work is comparable to Machiavelli's famous treatise, The Prince. His work is basically written for the King – in strengthening and establishing a more comprehensive and effective control system over land and population through laws and strict penalties. With a proper system of laws and well-defined punishments, all life within a nation will be in order, so that nothing would be left to chance, private judgement and the appeal to privilege (Watson, 1964). Besides, Han Fei Zi's writing also focuses on the art of governing – the delegation of power, the list of duties to be performed by his ministers, and the system of rewards and punishments. The art of governing espoused by Han Fei Zi is comparable to the modern management principle put forward by Henri Fayol.

The central idea of Han Fei Zi is that human by nature is evil – which is contrary to Confucius and Mencius' teachings. Han Fei Zi believed that peace and order of the nation is not an outcome of moral conduct but rather through laws and strict punishments. He does not endorse to education as a means to uplift the moral discipline of the individual. To Han Fei Zi, human being is guided solely by self-interest – even his own wife and children are not to be trusted.

The King of Qin strongly endorsed to and closely followed Han Fei Zi's school of thought. During his 14 years of ruling, he implemented several new systems, controlled the people with strict laws and suppressed the teachings of other schools of philosophy (Watson, 1964). However, he constantly lives in fear from being assassinated. Upon the death of the King of Qin in 207 B.C., the Qin dynasty was soon replaced by the Han dynasty three years later. Thereafter, no emperor or government in China ever followed wholesale the footsteps of the King of Qin, the Legalistic approach.

(a) The Wisdom of Using People

To Han Fei Zi, the highest ability of an organisational leader is not to display his own talents but to be able to attract talented people to work for him. This is the definition of an enlightened leader by Han Fei Zi. In this manner, though the leader may not worthy himself, he is the leader of the worthy. To be able to employ someone who more talented or capable than you to work for you is the finest ability of an enlightened leader.

"The ruler must not reveal his desires; for if he reveals his desires his ministers will put on the mask that pleases him. He must not reveal his will; for if he does so his ministers will show a different face. So it is said: Discard likes and dislikes and the ministers will show their true form; discard wisdom and wile and the ministers will watch their step. Hence, though the ruler is wise, he hatches no schemes from his wisdom, but causes all men to know their place. Though he has worth, he does not display it in his deeds, but observes the motives of his ministers. Though he is brave, he does not flaunt his bravery in shows of indignation, but allows his subordinates to display their valor to the full. Thus, though he discards wisdom, his rule is enlightened; though he discards worth, he achieves merit; and though he discards bravery, his state grows powerful. When the ministers stick to their posts, the hundred officials have their regular duties, and the ruler employs each according to his particular ability, this is known as the state of manifold constancy." (Section 5 of Han Fei Tzu – Watson, 1964)

According to Han Fei Zi (Section 5), they are five types of ministers that a ruler would not like to have:

(i) ministers that do not listen to the leader;

(ii) ministers that control the resources and wealth of the nation;

(iii) ministers that are free to issue order as they please;

(iv) ministers that do righteous deeds in their own name; and

(v) ministers that are capable to build their own cliques.

A wise leader is careful in assigning or delegating tasks to his subordinates without revealing his real motive to them. In this way, the leader can objectively evaluate the performance of his subordinate according to the way they have been carried out. If the accomplishments match the requirements of the tasks, rewards will be handed out. If things do not match, the subordinates will not receive any reward. By not rewarding is already a form of punishment.

If a leader shows his preferences or reveals his real motive in the beginning, then his subordinates will strive to put up a false frond just to please the leader. In such a case, the subordinates will never show their true colours and thus the leader will find it difficulty to distinguish between the able and the disable. It is when the subordinates have shown their true colour that the leader will not be deceived. Based on the words of Han Fei Zi in Section 7,

"Thus, if the ruler reveals what he dislikes, his ministers will be careful to disguise their motives; if he shows what he likes, his ministers will feign abilities they do not have. In short, if he lets his desires be known, he gives his ministers a clue as to what attitude they had best assume." (Watson, 1964)

In a knowledge economy, it is always difficult to attract talented people to work for one's company. But it is even more difficult to make them be committed and be loyal. As what Han Fei Zi said (in Section 12), *"It is not difficult to know a thing; what is difficult is to know how to use what you know."* (Watson, 1964). Thus, the most important thing to persuade and motivate one to contribute voluntarily is to know the mind of the person. For example, if you try to use money to motivate a person who has high aspiration, he will regard you as low-bred, and shabby. On the other hand, if you try to motivate a greedy person with high ideals or aspirations, he will regard you as witless and not realistic. Thus, a wise leader learns to first understand the mind of the subordinate and then find ways to match the need. To Han Fei Zi, the important thing a leader should do is to discuss things with the subordinate that he is proud of and play down things that his subordinate is ashamed of. A wise leader knows to stroke his subordinates in the right way.

Besides doing the right things, Han Fei Zi also highlighted ten faults that ruler should avoid (in Section 10, Watson, 1964):

(i) To practice petty loyalty and thereby betray a larger loyalty.

(ii) To fix your eye on a petty gain and thereby lose a larger one.

(iii) To behave in a base and wilful manner and show no courtesy to the other feudal lords, thereby bringing about your own downfall.

(iv) To give no ear to government affairs but long only for the sound of music, thereby plunging yourself into distress.

(v) To be greedy, perverse, and too fond of profit, thereby opening the way to the destruction of the state and your own demise.

(vi) To become infatuated with women musicians and disregard state affairs, thereby inviting the disaster of national destruction.

(vii) To leave the palace for distant travels, despising the remonstrance of your minister, which lead to grave peril for yourself.

(viii) To fail to heed you loyal ministers when you are at fault, insisting upon having your own way, which will in time destroy your good reputation and make you a laughing stock of others.

(ix) To take no account of internal strength and rely solely upon your allies abroad, which places the state in grave danger of dismemberment.

(x) To ignore the demands of courtesy, though your sate is small, and fail to learn from the remonstrance of your ministers, acts which lead to the downfall of your line.

The 'Art of Rulership' is similar to the art of relationship between the ruler and the subjects. To Han Fei Zi, the bond of loyalty which can exists between ruler and subject and the execution of this bond as an effective means of ensuring diligent and faithful service from the subject (Ames, 1983). To Han Fei Zi, the relationship between a ruler and his subjects was based on a mutually cooperative and beneficial relationship rather than mutual obligations and responsibilities.

If a ruler does not entrust things to the capable but instead handled himself, he will ultimately tax himself with too much responsibility. Besides, his ministers will hide their intelligence and thus passing the burden to the ruler instead. In this manner, the intelligence of the ministers will not be put into good use. The role of a ruler is to identify the right person to do the right job. This is the wisdom of using people.

Although the way to rule a country may differs slightly from leading an organisation, the basic management principle remains relatively similar. Similarly, the way of leading in ancient times may differ from today's circumstances, but the fundamentals are still relatively unchanged. A wise leader knows to keep an eye on the long-term horizon but would never forget to keep at least a shadow of the ancient wisdom.

(b) The Concept of Discipline

To Han Fei Zi, if the people are fearful of "being disciplined", he will act morally to avoid them. The fear of "being disciplined" may not be a bad thing. Fear of being disciplined (the control orientation) will bring about good behaviour (the 'goodness'). Thus a wise leader is able to embrace the 'goodness' and 'badness' of things. By embracing the 'good' and the 'bad' guys, the wise leader uses the characteristics of the 'good' guy such as his honesty and humanity to carry out his duties while he could use the characteristics of the 'bad' guy such as his greed to do some of the so-called 'dirty' jobs.

A wise leader is able to balance between strictness with leniency. Before one could discipline others, he must first be able to discipline himself. This is an instant of 'Leadership by example'. According to Han Fei Zi (in Section 6), for those who uphold the law, the state will be strong. To the legalist, the best way to prevent or deter crime is to have harsh laws, that is, heavy punishment for any form of violation. Although having harsh laws are against the principle of humility espoused in Confucianism, the legalist argued that **prevention is better cure**. Moreover, if the punishment is made severe enough, it will be hardly be used as nobody or very few people will dare to break the law. Han Fei Zi said,

"If the ruler of men tries to keep a personal check on all the various offices of his government, he will find the day too short and his energies insufficient. Moreover if a ruler uses his eyes, his subordinates will try to beautify what he sees; if he uses his ears, they will try to embellish what he hears; and if he uses his mind they will be at him with endless speeches. The former kings, knowing that these faculties would not suffice, accordingly set aside their own abilities; instead they relied upon law and policy, and took care to see that rewards and punishments were correctly apportioned. Since they held fast to the essential point, their legal codes were simple and yet inviolable, and alone they exercised control over all within the four seas." (quoted from "The Great Thoughts of China by Liang Congjie, page 132).

Fundamentally, the key characteristic of the ancient Chinese legal system was based on duty rather than rights, although there are two inter-related concepts. Besides, the legal system of the ancient Chinese is an intertwined concept of law and morality. Based on the legalists like Shang Yang, if the country is governs by penal laws, the people will fear and thus will not commit crimes. In this manner, people will be moral or ethical and the multitude will enjoy peace and prosperity. Shang Yang, Han Fei Zi and Li Si (the Prime Minister of the Qin emperor) were fully subscribed to the School of Legalism.

When Li Si was appointed as the Prime Minister of the Qin

empire (a new empire), he put into practise the system of legalism by:

- Putting in place a single unified administration with centralization of power and regimentation of its people (based on a strict division of labour);
- Providing a new sense of unity and nationalism by putting the entire China under the direct control of the central court;
- Wiping out all feudal ranks and took away all their privileges;
- Standardizing of weights, measures and writing.
- Ruling people by strict laws and harsh penalties.

Upon the death of Qin emperor, Li Si and his family was subsequently destroyed by the eunuch, Zhao Gao using the legalistic method that he had employed. Zhao Gao was very much valued by Emperor Qin ShiHuang as he was an expert in law and punishment. Three years after the death of Emperor Qin ShiHuang, Zhao was killed and the entire Qin Dynasty was surrendered to Liu Bang, the first emperor of the Han dynasty. In fact, all the three leading legalists, Shang Yang, Han Fei Zi and Li Si as well as eunuch Zhao Gao ended their lives tragically.

The following are some tenets of Han Fei Zi's philosophy (Sheh, 1998) and the Legalist interpretation of penal law (Ames, 1983):

(i) Good laws are a necessary condition for proper social order. A ruler without laws is the same as no ruler. A ruler's position in any matter is always justified by his power to reward and punish. Thus, he should not share too much of his power to reward and punish with his ministers. A ruler should rule his people through the exercise of his authority and the administering of laws.

(ii) Penal laws are impartial. Whatever that is in accordance to the law is considered good; and whatever that is not in accordance to the law is considered bad. Those who violate the laws should be punished; those who obey the laws should be rewarded. Man is self-seeking by nature. Hence, man's conduct needs to be guarded by law and codes of behaviour.

(iii) In the eyes of the law, all men are equal, regardless of their status or influence. Only the ruler himself is beyond the law. Not even the prince, is above the law.

(iv) In formulating the law, the penalty for breaking that law has to be severe to deter anyone from violating the law. The laws need to be periodically reviewed and change in order to meet and reflect the changing environment. After formulation, it should ideally be made known and fully understood by all members of the society.

(v) In implementing the law, there must be absolute enforcement. No man must be considered to be above the law.

Adapting from the book entitled, "*The Art of Rulership*" (by Ames, 1983), in line with the penal law, the quality of the government or ruler can be divided into 3 levels as follows:

Highest level: *"The highest ruler is godlike in his transformations. The most desirable level of government is one in which the charismatic influence of the ruler has transformed the people such that they do what is right of their own accord."*

Second level: *"One who makes it impossible for people to do wrong. The government is one in which control consists solely in prohibiting actions which threaten social and political harmony."*

Lowest level: *"One who rewards those of superior qualities and punishes the troublemakers. The government telling the people what they should and should not do by establishing a system of incentives and deterrents."*

In enforcement, it is important to get the right person in place. The person-in-charge should have clear understanding of what is beneficial to the nation and what is not, and familiar with the system of laws and regulations. For example, in some countries they are many laws being passed by the parliament on anti-corruption, but yet the officials are still highly corrupted. In such cases, the officials have turned their backs on the law in pursuing their personal benefits. This will ultimately bring chaos and disorder to the nation – that explains the backwardness of some countries.

In the organisational context, rules and regulations that have been approved should not be disputed and be properly enforced. When someone violated the rules or regulations, even the CEO of the company cannot be spared. However, in meting out the punishment, it is commonly for the Chinese organisation to practice the steps of three R that is Relationship, Reason and Reprimand.

In meting out punishment, the Chinese leader would consider the "qing 情 " (relationship/feeling of others) will take precedence followed by "li 理 " (reasoning) then only "fa 法 " (reprimand). Before meting out the punishment, consideration should be given to the relationship between the employer and the employee. After the **relationship** has been considered, then the company should consider reason – that is the **reason** or rationale behind the mistake. If both relationship and reason have been taken into consideration, then the company will mete out the type of **reprimand** to be imposed.

(c) The Use of Reward and Punishment

According to Han Fei Zi, an enlightened ruler controls his ministers using two types of power; power to reward and power to punish. If a ruler loses control over these two powers, then he will be in danger.

"The tiger is able to overpower the dog because of his claws and teeth, but if he discards his claws and teeth and lets the dog use them, then on the contrary he will overpowered by the dog. In the same way the ruler of men uses punishments and favors to control his ministers, but if he discards his punishments and favors and lets his ministers employ them, then on the contrary he will find himself in the control of his ministers." (Section 7- Watson, 1964)

If a leader does not possess the power to reward and punish, just like a tiger loses its claws and teeth, then he will lose his power to influence his subordinates. Let me use a hypothetical example to illustrate my point. Once upon a time, there was a King who asked his Prime Minister to see him. When the Prime Minister arrived, he told the Prime Minister that: *"From today onwards, I will do all the rewarding and you will do all the punishing"*. Since then, the King starts to reward people who do the right things while the Prime Minister was well-known for punishing people who makes mistakes. Naturally, over time, everybody is afraid of the Prime Minister. However, subsequently, the Prime Minister started to change his strategy – he started to be lenient and spared some people from severe punishments. Over the years, many people were spared by the Prime Minister and felt very grateful to the Prime Minister. When the Prime Minister has gathered sufficient supporters, he overthrown the King and made himself the King. The morale of the story is that though the King only delegated one of his two powers to the Prime Minister, he lost his empire in the end. On the other hand, though the Prime Minister only being empowered to punish, he knows how to use the power wisely. To the Prime Minister, not punishing is also a form of reward. Thus, the Prime Minister has able to overcome the King and finally becomes the King himself.

In meting out rewards and punishments, the leader never overdoing it. In Section 5 of Han Fei Zi;

"... The enlightened ruler is never over liberal in his rewards, never over lenient in his punishments. If his rewards are too liberal, then ministers who have won merit in the past will grow lax in their duties; and if his punishments are too lenient, then evil ministers will find it easy to do wrong. Thus if a man has truly won merit, no matter how humble and far removed he may be, he must be rewarded; and if he has truly committed error, no matter how close and clear to the ruler he may be, he must be punished. If those who are humble and far removed can be sure of reward, and those close and clear to the ruler can be sure of punishment, then the former will not stint in their efforts and the latter will not grow proud." (Watson, 1964)

Whatever is regarded as right should be adopted in administration while whatever is regarded as wrong should be eliminated, or-else the world will be in chaos (De bary, 1960). Basically, power can be divided into two major types that are power to reward and power to punish. To the legalist, the power to punish is the best strategy to use to govern a country. It is because the legalist believed human is by nature evil. As such, it is through laws and punishments, that human will be good. Han Fei Zi said,

"The law no more makes exceptions for men of high station than the plumb line bends to accommodate a crooked place in the wood. What the law has decreed the wise man cannot dispute nor the brave man venture to contest. When faults are to be punished, the highest minister cannot escape; when good is to be rewarded, the lowest peasant must not be passed over." (quoted from "The Great Thoughts of China" by Liang Congjie, page 115, 1996).

There is a Chinese saying that goes thus: *"We need to punish the one in order to warn the hundreds"*. In other words, the Chinese leader believes that in order to ensure the effectiveness of the law, he must enforce it by punishing the few so as to warn the multitude that the law – and its enforcement – is real. On the other hand, Confucius believed man to be by nature kind and good. The Confucianists maintain that people should be ruled by proper rules of conduct and morality.

Based on the assumption that man's nature is good, one would be able to cultivate a person's character and train one's personality through proper education, both at home and in school (Sheh, 1998).

Having harsh laws and regulations with strict enforcement may not be a bad thing. At times, it is important to conform to the "Thick Black Theory" - Thick Face, Black Heart (Chu, 2005). It is essential for an effective leader to be a disciplinarian. However, the human aspect should not be overlooked. If an effective legal system alone can manage and control human behaviours, there would be no crime. Although effective laws and rules are important in guiding human behaviour, they do not automatically make people more moral or ethical. A truly effective leader is able to balance compassion and benevolence with strict and harsh laws.

CHAPTER 3
RULERSHIP

The Chinese culture is the longest shared culture on earth. The Chinese writing system was only found about 4,000 years ago through the discovery by archaeologists of writings inscribed on bones. The Chinese started to develop the ability to make pottery to store food and drink about 4,000 to 5,000 years ago. It was over 2,000 years ago that the imperial dynastic system of government was first formed. Between 770 and 221 BC, China experienced the long period of the warring states – approximately 550 years. It was during this chaotic period that several great philosophers, Lao Zi, Confucius, Mozi, Mencius, Zhuang Zi, Xunzi and Han Fei Zi were born. In the Chinese community there is a proverb that says, “It is the right environment that creates the hero and not the hero who creates the environment”. Thus, when China was in a chaotic period, great thinkers were born.

The first imperial dynastic system of government was the Qin dynasty established by Qin ShiHuang in 221 BC. Since then, many dynasties were overturned. However, the dynastic system survived for 2,132 years until it was finally overturned in 1911 and a republican form of government existed until 1949. For over 2,132 years, China was ruled by two foreign invaders namely, the Mongols (from AD 1279 to 1368 for 90 years) and the Manchus (from AD 1644 to 1911 for 267 years). The Qing dynasty collapsed in 1911 and was taken over by revolutionaries, the National Party led by Dr. Sun Yat-Sen. The Communist Party emerged in 1921 and a civil war between the National Party and the Communist Party took place in 1927 until

1936. The Japanese invaded China in 1937, which sparked off an anti-Japanese war until 1945. Finally, the People's Republic of China was founded in 1949 by Mao Zedong. A summary of the Chinese Chronology is as per Table 3.1.

Table 3.1
A Summary of Chinese History

Number of Years	Dates	Dynasties
500	2100 – 1600 BC	Xia
500	1600 – 1100 BC	Shang
330	1100 – 771 BC	Western Zhou
550	770 – 221 BC	Eastern Zhou, Spring & Autumn Period and Warring States
14	221 – 207 BC	Qin (1st Emperor of China)
426	206 BC – 220 AD	Han – Western and Eastern
60	220 – 280 AD	Three Kingdoms
155	265 – 420 AD	Jin – Western and Eastern
161	420 – 581 AD	Northern and Southern
37	581 – 618 AD	Sui
289	618 – 907 AD	Tang
53	907 – 960 AD	Five Dynasties
319	960 – 1279 AD	Sung – Northern and Southern
209	916 – 1125 AD	Liao
119	1115 – 1234 AD	Jin
90	1279 – 1368 AD	Yuan (Mongolian)
276	1368 – 1644 AD	Ming
267	1644 – 1911 AD	Qing (Manchurian)
37	1912 – 1949 AD	Republic of China
	1949 - todate	People's Republic of China

Based on a review of the Chinese rulers and governments over the past 4,000 years, the following rulers or governments were highlighted:

- King Xuan of Qi (about 302 BC);
- Chancellor of Qin, Shang Yang (3rd BC) in 'the Book of Lord Shang';
- Emperor Qin ShiHuang (221 – 206 BC); and
- Emperor Wu Di (156-87 BC) of the Han Dynasty who applied Confucian ideals with soft Legalist practices.

KING XUAN OF QI (about 302 BC)

King Xuan of Qi used the works of Guan Zhong in governing the state. Guan Zhong (born in 723 BC and died in 645 BC) was the Prime Minister of Duke Huan of Qi in 685 BC (during the Spring and Autumn period). During Guan Zhong's tenure, he carried out several political and administration reforms such as (source: Wikipedia):

(a) Divide and rule: he divided the state into different villages while power was centralized at the state.

(b) Recruitment: with respect to recruiting people, he used professional bureaucrats instead of relying on the traditional aristocracy (which was based on heredity).

(c) Economic reform: he introduced a uniform tax reform to collect revenue for the state. He also introduced state monopolies for the salt and iron industries.

Guan Zhong's works were compiled around 3rd century BC by the Jixia Academy and was called the "Guanzi". Guan Zhong's works were considered the forerunner of Legalism. In about 302 BC, King Xuan of Qi used the "Guanzi" to govern the state. To King Xuan, a good and successful government depended on:

(a) Providing the economic needs of the people through cultivation of grains, horticulture and rearing of domestic animals. In addition, a good government opens up fields for cultivation, regulates shops, builds roads as well as facilitates market transactions.

(b) Employing those with skills to execute orders, give consistent rewards to encourage the people and mete out stern punishments to those who commit crimes. In terms of rewards, top officials were given high incentives to influence those who worked for them.

(c) Laws and regulations were used to maintain social order. In addition, laws established the authority of the government. The use of collective responsibility for crimes instead of individual responsibility greatly deterred people from committing wrongdoings. Under collective responsibility, the responsibility for crimes extended upward in the hierarchy from members to the head of the family, village, sub-district, district and finally to the chief justice.

The ultimate aim of "Guanzi" was to advice the government on how to make the people happy.

CHANCELLOR OF QIN, SHANG YANG (3rd Century BC)

Shang Yang (born in 390BC and died in 338 BC) was the chancellor of Duke Xiao of Qin. He was known to be a major legalist thinker and statesman. Shang Yang's political strategy was to create a centralized political system through a team of chosen governors with standardized administration. With the support of Duke Xiao of Qin, Shang Yang implemented a series of reforms that changed the Qin state into a militarily powerful and centralized kingdom. Some of his reforms include:

(a) Implemented the Book of Law (also known as Li Kui's Book of Law). Although various forms of laws had existed during the Spring and Autumn period, Shang Yang studied and put them into practice. Shang Yang studied law when he was young. His legalistic approach was faced with strong opposition from many Confucian scholars. Despite all the oppositions, he still spread the knowledge of law among all officials.

(b) Created a high hierarchy among the military (up to 20 military ranks or levels). His key aim was to reinforce the importance of battlefield success and the formation of a powerful military force. Shang Yang subscribed to military merit – where reward and punishment would be based on objective measurable performance. This has become the foundation that enabled Qin to conquer all of China, putting an end to the warring states and uniting the country for the first time under the Qin dynasty in 221 BC.

(c) Introduced land reforms by allowing farmers to own their lands and rewarding farmers that met government policies, such as farmers who cultivated wasteland. As part of the farmers had been asked to join the military, Shang Yang implemented a foreign immigration policy allowing the immigration of peasants from other states to strengthen the workforce. Shang Yang believed that having a large population was a pre-requisite for a strong nation.

Shang Yang's legacy was presented in the 'Book of Lord Shang' where part of the writing was composed after his death. His views and major concerns were to assist the ruler to control the people through rules and laws. To Shang Yang, the people were inherently selfish and ignorant and thus, the best way to maintain social order is through enactment of a uniform legal system supported by a reward and punishment system.

Punishments had to be severe by imposing harsh penalties for violations of the law and thus, preventing people from wrongdoings (subscribed to "prevention is better than cure"). This is the best way to ensure that the people will ultimately act morally. To Shang Yang, everybody was equal under the law. On the other hand, he believed in using an effective reward system to encourage people to work hard. He disagreed that it was the cultivation of virtue that made people work hard. In executing rewards, they should be based on merit and measurable performance instead of the seniority or nobility of people. Thus, he subscribed to the 'principle of meritocracy'.

EMPEROR QIN SHI HUANG (秦始皇)- 221-201 BC

Before the establishment of China's first dynasty by Emperor Shi Huang, China experienced 550 years of the Warring States – from an age of relative peace to one of chaos. It was also during this period of frequent wars that two great philosophers, Lao Tzu and Confucius, as well as thegreat military specialist, Sun Tzu (the author of the Art of War), were born. During the Warring States period there were seven principal states – Chu, Han, Qi, Qin, Wei, Yan and Zhao. Among the seven states, the State of Qin was the most dynamic one. The King of the Qin state, Yingzheng (or better known as Qin ShiHuang), conquered the other six states through ten years of wars and brought an end to the Warring States in 221 BC. He built up the Qin Dynasty, the first centralized autocratic and feudal dynasty in China, making Xianyang the capital city. After the unification of China, Emperor Qin ShiHuang was the first to use the title "emperor" (the First Emperor of China) but ruled China for a short period of 11 years. The Qin Dynasty only lasted for 15 years – this started the 2,000-year dynastic system in China. Thereafter, the title "emperor" became the exclusive title for all rulers of the dynastic system in China.

Yingzheng (259-210 BC), son of King Zhuangxiang of the state Qin, took over from his father at the age of 13. After Yingzheng succeeded the throne, his mother, Zhao Ji became Empress Dowager and made Lu Buwei the Prime Minister. Between the age of 13 and 22, Yingzheng's administration of the country was under the control of the Prime Minister, Lu Buwei. When, Yingzheng gathered sufficient strength, he sentenced the prime minister to jail, where he subsequently poisoned himself to death, and Yingzheng launched his unification campaign from 230 BC to 221 BC. He started to recruit and employ men of talent to serve him. His eagerness to employ capable and talented people made him a model for future generations to follow. After Yingzheng achieved internal consolidation and stability, his vision was to conquer the other six states and unite them into one country. It is this ambitious aim and determination that saw Yingzheng eventually manage to "swallow" all the six states in 10 years and declare himself as the first emperor of China. It was Yingzheng's goal to bring about eternal peace that caused him to embark on 10 years of wars.

Emperor Qin was a great politician as well as a visionary leader. Although his merits and demerits brought him a lot of praise and blame – he was by no means a remarkable emperor. Besides his strong and compelling vision to unite China, he was a transformational leader. During the 11 years of rule by Emperor Qin, after the founding of the Qin Dynasty, he made several major reforms:

- Re-designing of the political organization and structure.
- Unification of currency, weights and measures.
- Standardization of the writing system.
- Construction of the Great Wall.

Redesigning of the Political Organization and Structure

Emperor Qin created three key positions to assist him in the administration of the country; the Prime Minister, the Military Commissioner and the Imperial Supervisor. The main duty of the Prime Minister was to assist the Emperor in managing the country, while the duty of the Military Commissioner was to take charge of military affairs. The duty of the Imperial Supervisor was to supervise Court Officials. He then departmentalized the political structure into 9 departments with each department respectively in charge of:

- Religious rites
- Royal families
- Palace affairs
- Palace security
- Carriages and tours

- Prisons
- Financial and treasury matters
- Foreign affairs and minority interests
- Royal financial affairs

The country was then further divided into 36 prefectures with each prefecture administered by three officers. Each prefecture was sub-divided into a few counties and further sub-divided into townships and villages (called the local government). Thus, the entire administration was formed from the central government to the local government. This divisional and sub-divisional structure (principle of divide and rule) was to prevent any potential revolt from the former six kingdoms as well as to facilitate tighter control.

Unification of Currency, Weights and Measures

After a centralized structure and system had been fully installed, Emperor Qin started to make economic and social changes. Before the unification of China, each of the 7 kingdoms had their own currencies with various shapes, sizes and weights – some shaped like a knife while others had round-shaped coins. This made trading among the seven kingdoms tedious and inefficient. Thus, Emperor Qin abolished the use of the seven different currencies and replaced it with a new monetary system based on two basic currencies – gold as one unit of currency and a round copper coin with a square hole in the centre as the other. Besides using different currencies, the weights and measures also differed among the seven kingdoms. Again, Emperor Qin replaced the different weights and measures with a system adopted by the Qin state.

Standardisation of the Writing System

After introducing a centralized political structure and system, Emperor Qin intended to consolidate his position further by uniting the minds of the Chinese. In the past, each of the states spoke different dialects and wrote differently, which hindered effective communication among the states. In order to standardize the writing system, a standardized script was created.

In order to standardize human thought and prevent people from criticizing the government by quoting the classics, he ordered all history books of the various states, Confucian books and other literature books to be burned. This was to reduce or even eliminate any form of criticism that did not conform with the legalistic school of thought. After the book-burning exercise, the Emperor started to bury scholars alive. Hundreds of philosophies and philosophers were destroyed. As a result, he was labeled a ruthless tyrant.

Construction of the Great Wall

When referring to the Great Wall of China, we often relate it to Emperor Qin ShiHuang – the person who planned the construction of the Great Wall. During the Qin Dynasty, China only had a population of around 20 million whereby half a million were deployed to take part in the construction of the Great Wall. After Emperor Qin successfully conquered all the six states, in order to strengthen his victory and to protect against the invasion of neighboring tribes and countries, he decided to construct the Great Wall. It took more than 10 years of hard labor to connect the original walls in Yan, Zhao and Qin, stretching from Lanzhou to Liaodong in the east – the total length being over 10,000 li. The Great Wall was subsequently restored during the Ming Dynasty.

During his 11 years of rule after the unification of China, Emperor Qin devoted a lot of his time and effort in attending to the state affairs. He would read piles of reports and attend to all documents personally. However, he ruled the country using ruthless means. During the Qin Dynasty, heavy taxes and harsh laws were introduced. Emperor Qin's political philosophy was very much influenced by the philosopher, Han Fei Tzu – who defined human nature as evil and thus, harsh laws and punishments were required. As a result of ruthless exploitation in the Qin Dynasty, many people lived in misery and struggled for mere existence.

In order to consolidate the seven kingdoms and bring peace and stability to united China, Emperor Qin endorsed using force as a means to rule by introducing an effective legal system – ruling with an iron fist. Besides constructing the Great Wall as self-defense, he also conducted massive military campaigns and built a strong military force. Finally, riots broke out and the Qin Dynasty was toppled after it existed for 15 years (till 207 BC). Liu Bang successfully managed to defeat the Qin Dynasty and formed the Han Dynasty in 206 BC. Although the Qin Dynasty only lasted for 15 years, the impact created by Qin ShiHuang in China was great, such as the 'Construction of the Great Wall' and the 'Burning of Books'.

In evaluating the rise and fall of the Qin Dynasty, the success factors of Emperor Qin include his foresight and vision, his strong execution power and his eagerness to employ talented people to work for him. In order to attract talented people, he would reward them handsomely with high-ranking offices and land. Besides, he also possessed the ability to plan and introduce change in a large scale. Although the tenure of the Qin dynasty was short-lived it served as a turning point in Chinese history. It provided the ancient Chinese with a new sense of unity and nationalism. Upon the death of Emperor Qin, the weaknesses of legalism started to be revealed.

The ruthlessness and heinous deeds of the Emperor Qin led to his downfall. When the second emperor of Qin took over the throne, he was unable to perform and was forced to commit suicide. After the downfall of the Qin Dynasty, although many dynasties were created thereafter, none of the rulers adopted his ruthless way of ruling. The Han Empire continued to unite China using a more gradual and peaceful means. In fact, later emperors used a more benevolent way of ruling based on the philosophy and teaching of Confucius - that is by defining human nature as naturally good. Thus, moral values and education were strongly emphasized in the development of a man.

"Good government will be blessed with good results; Misgovernment will bring about misfortune."

EMPEROR WU DI (武帝)- 156-87 BC

Emperor Wu Di (武帝) (156 – 87 BC), the fifth emperor of the Western Han Dynasty, Liu Che (刘彻) is remembered as a fighting emperor. With his superior ability coupled with his extraordinarily high courage and propensity for risk, he engaged in a prolonged struggle with the Huns for over 44 years (from 134 BC to 91 BC). When Liu Che ascended the throne, society was enjoying peace and prosperity. But he was not contented with things as they were. To further unite China after the Qin Dynasty, Liu Che launched many wars against the aggressive Huns who had posed security threats to the Han Dynasty for many years at the northern frontier.

Although Qin Shi Huang built the Great Wall to defend the northern frontier, it was no longer enough to defend against the nomad attacks from those known as the Xiongnu (the Huns). His attacks against the Huns were so aggressive that he did not allow the Huns to recuperate. In addition, Liu Che also implemented several other measures to further unify and improve China.

- Summoned all the scholars and promoted talented people to make the Han Dynasty even more prosperous.
- Implemented policy to regulate transport and control prices to prevent monopoly by big merchants.
- Implemented monetary policy and control.
- Weakened the political influence of princes bearing the royal surname.
- Repaired the Huzi breach to prevent floods of the Yellow River.

The Qualities of a Legalistic Leader

Based on the literature review of the works of Xunzi and Han Fei Zi as well as the ancient rulers who practiced high levels of legalism and bureaucracy, a list of behavioral characteristics of the Chinese legalistic leader was developed. The Chinese legalistic leader:

- emphasizes on absolute enforcement, where no man must be considered above the law and rule, including the Crown Prince. In order to sustain a country's long-term prosperity, installing an effective and comprehensive legal system should take priority over having good people.
- uses the penal code as an instrument of political administration. The legalistic ruler should first prevent the people from doing wrong before encouraging them to do good.
- exercises strict discipline, yet is impartial (fair). The legalistic leader favors enforcing discipline, rules and regulations. He maintains good self-discipline before disciplining others. Laws must be strictly enforced. He should continuously review the laws to ensure that they are relevant to the changing conditions.
- is careful in delegating tasks to his subordinates without revealing his real motives. In this manner, the subordinates would be unable to put on a 'mask' in front of the leader.
- believes that punishment must be harsh or severe enough to serve as deterrent (prevention is better than cure).
- implements high degrees of bureaucracy to ensure the smooth functioning of an orderly organization which includes installing a ranked hierarchy, instituting a centralized power, enforcing a rule-based code of conduct, and implementing a punitive system that instills fear in others and thus, achieves high levels of obedience.
- does not display his own talents but is able to attract talented people to work for him. The legalistic leader subscribes to an effective reward system to encourage the capable to act, while also subscribing to a comprehensive punishment system to deter any form of deviant behavior.

- is beyond praise or criticism from others. When praised, he is not elated. When criticized, he is not easily agitated.

Some of the characteristics of an ineffective or bad Chinese legalistic leader or ruler are:

- He is unable to differentiate between what is right and what is wrong.
- He is unable to identify and employ worthy people.
- He is unable to promote the most deserving people for a higher position and responsibility.
- He is unable to execute the laws and punish the wrong-doers.
- He is unable or unwilling to share his credits with his subordinates.
- He is unable to take responsibility of his own failures.

As said by Napoleon, a leader is a dealer in hope. Leadership can be defined as to lead and to follow – to **lead** the people to a higher level of excellence by **following** the wishes of his people. The key aim of a wise ruler or government is to serve.

Some Quotations on Ruler-ship

**"Inferior ruler makes full use of his own talents;
Average ruler makes full use of the strength of others; and
Superior ruler makes full use of the intelligence of others."**

Ames, "The Art of Rulership", 1983

**"The worst is the one despised by the people.
The third best is the one feared by the people.
The second best is the one praised by the people.
The best government does not make its presence felt."**

Michael C. Tang, "A Victor's Reflections", 2000

Based on the review of the different schools of thought: the Humanistic, Legalistic and Naturalistic schools of thought in Chinese literature, a ruler can be classified into at least three types:

The Worst Leader/Ruler

If a leader or ruler seeks to "rule" his people, he will formulate rules and regulations and enforce them to maintain control. Once people feel they are being controlled and cannot act according to their free will or desires, they will naturally rebel. This will result in the leader or ruler imposing more rules and regulations to control the people. In the end, the people will rebel more and society will be in chaos. A weak leader is easy to bully, while a strong leader is difficult to please. A leader who takes advantage of his power will also take advantage of his people. This type of ruler is very much based on the **School of Legalism**.

"A wise leader does not reveal his desires. If a leader reveals his likes and dislikes, the subordinates will put on a mask to please the leader.

A wise leader is beyond praise or criticism. When praised, he is not elated. When criticized, he is not easily agitated."

The Average Leader/Ruler

The average leader or ruler would circumscribe his people with social values and norms and enforce these through education to maintain control. In this manner, the people would be subtly suppressed to conform to these values and norms – so-called civilization. Again, this does not allow the people to live according to their free will. This type of ruler is very much based on the **School of Humanism**.

"If you want one year of prosperity, grow grains.
If you want ten years of prosperity, grow trees.
If you want one hundred years of prosperity, grow PEOPLE."
- Chinese proverb

The Best Leader/Ruler

The best type of leader or ruler does not "rule" his people, and yet society is peaceful and harmonious. This leader or ruler would gently and subtly lead the people through his actions and allow the people to express themselves according to their free will. The best leader or ruler strives for nothing, says nothing, and does nothing. In this manner, everybody lives according to the Way – the Principle of No Action or Least Action. This type of ruler is very much from the **School of Naturalism**.

"The best of all rulers is but a shadowy presence to his subjects.
When his task is accomplished and his work done,
the people all say,
'It happened to us naturally.'"
(Chapter 17 of Dao De Jing, Lau, 1963)

CHAPTER 4
THE WESTERN LEGAL AND POLITICAL SYSTEM

LEGAL SYSTEM OF THE WORLD

The national legal system varies from one country to another. The rule of law, the role of lawyers and judges, the burden of proof, the judicial process and the laws themselves differ from country to country. The world legal system can be briefly categorized into civil law, common law, religious law, and bureaucratic law.

1. Civil Law

Civil law is the world's most common type of legal system. It is based on a detailed listing of 'what is and what is not permissible'. Civil law is based on a set of written rules and statutes that constitute a legal code. The concept of codification can be traced back to as early as the Code of Hammurabi in Babylon around 1700 BC. Under civil law, all obligations, responsibilities and privileges follow the code. In enforcing the law, the judge takes on many of the tasks of the lawyers, such as determining the scope of evidence to be collected and presented to the Court. Some of the countries that practice civil law include France, Germany, Austria, Switzerland, Denmark, Norway and Sweden (among the European countries) as well as Asian countries like Japan, South Korea and even China (which combines civil law with bureaucratic/socialist law).

2. Common Law

Common law was developed in England. Basically, a common legal system reflects three factors:
- Tradition – a country's legal history.
- Precedent – past cases that have come before the Court.
- Usage – the way in which laws are applied in specific situations.

Each case may be interpreted differently. Thus, business contracts tend to be lengthy in order to cover as many possible interpretations of the law that may apply in case of disputes. The positive side of common law systems is its flexibility because the laws take into account the particular situations of the case. Some of the countries that practice Common Law include UK, USA, Australia, New Zealand, Canada, India, Singapore and Malaysia,

3. Religious Law

The main kinds of religious law are Sharia in Islam and Halakha in Judaism. A country that applies religious law is called a theocracy. Some of the countries that practice Islamic law include Afghanistan, Saudi Arabia, Iran, Libya, Sudan and Yemen, just to name a few.

4. Bureaucratic Law

Bureaucratic law was a common practice among communist countries and in dictatorships. Bureaucratic law is whatever the country's bureaucrat would dictate. In the past, China practiced bureaucratic law (between 1949 and 1979) but is currently undergoing a major legal reform to civil law. Currently, China practices a mixture of civil law and socialist law.

BUREAUCRATIC STATE

Max Weber (1864-1920) put forward in his work "Economy and Society" the political philosophy of the bureaucratic state in governing an economy. His work mainly focuses on:

1. The distribution of power being commensurate with the duties given.
2. The hiring of qualified officials to join the government.
3. The importance of hierarchy and the authority structure.
4. The development of a written set of rules that is to be universally enforced.
5. The principle of specialization to ensure the right person is given the right job.

The above will ultimately lead to greater level of efficiency in managing the resources of a nation. In the long term, it will lead to greater prosperity for the country.

EVOLUTION OF WESTERN LEGAL PHILOSOPHY

Western legal philosophers hope to obtain a deeper understanding of the nature of law, of legal reasoning, legal systems and legal institutions. Basically, legal study has evolved from natural law to legal positivism to legal realism. Based on Wikipedia (in 2010), the following information was extracted and is discussed here.

1. Natural Law

Aristotle (384 BC – 322 BC) was a Greek philosopher, who is often said to be the father of natural law which is based on human reasoning. Aristotle's theory of justice refers to two different but related ideas: general justice and particular justice, whereby particular justice is a sub-set of general justice. General justice often refers to all matters in relation to others, while particular justice refers to treating others in an equitable manner. Aristotle's idea of right and wrong is very much focused on morality rather than a system of laws. His ideas on morality are comparable to Confucius (551 – 479 BC) in China.

2. Legal Positivism

Legal positivism derives laws from some basic social facts to provide a written set of rules that will ensure social order and good governance of society. One of the earliest legal positivists was Jeremy Bentham in the $18^{th}/19^{th}$ century.

3. Legal Realism

Legal realism believes that law can only be understood through actual practice. This view was made popular by some Scandinavian and American scholars. This concept of legal realism is still more commonly subscribed to by legal practitioners and scholars especially in the United States.

Today, legal philosophers continue to deliberate much on questions such as "What is law?", "What is the purpose of law?", "What are the moral principles or values behind the formation of law?", "What is justice?" and so on. When someone makes a mistake or commits a crime, is our action to punish or to take revenge? In order to justify punishment, we need to first define what is wrongdoing. Law is made by human beings and thus, subject to imperfections as human beings themselves are not perfect.

THE POLITICAL TREATISE OF NICCOLO MACHIAVELLI

Niccolo Machiavelli, born in 1469, was an Italian public servant who wrote the book entitled, "The Prince", which was only published five years after his death in 1532. Machiavelli started work as a secretary for the government of Florence and was soon engaged in diplomatic missions where he met many important politicians and members of the royal families. When Machiavelli was dismissed from office with the coming of Medici rule in Florence, he switched to writing about politics.

Machiavelli lived in a period of political turmoil. His political writing was to advice the prince on how to maintain social order through building up the prince's reputation. Some of the key tenets of "The Prince" are (extracted from Wikipedia):

- A capable prince puts great emphasis on developing his own military power instead of relying on his allies. Even if he has no intention to attack other territories, he should at all times be prepared for his country to defend itself.
- A prince should learn to control his expenditure by avoiding being too generous and overspending. It is far better for the prince to be labeled as a miser than as extravagant.
- A prince should possess some of the good qualities of a leader that includes being merciful, humane and faithful. He should always keep his word and thus be perceived by his people as reliable. However, at times, it is unavoidable that a prince may have to play the role of a bad guy in order to maintain his position, especially in dealing with difficult people.
- A prince should use his intelligence in selecting the right people to work for him especially in recruiting loyal staff. In judging people, a wise prince should be able to distinguish between good and bad people.

- A prudent prince should know how to seek the advice of his counselors before making a decision. In addition, he should possess the wisdom to distinguish between good and bad advice.

- A great prince relies on his own intelligence and effort to establish his position. He should never depend on luck. A prince who lacks ability will not be able to sustain his position for long.

- A prince needs to impose fear in his people but not to the extent of hatred. In this manner, he will gain the respect of his people and yet they will not rebel.

- A prince must be assertive. When he needs to make a choice, he should not stay neutral. He should also be bold enough to make his choice and then be courageous enough to pursue it.

In contemporary times, "The Prince" can be applied to governing a country as well as managing an organization, particularly in respect to 'political structure', 'chain of command', 'control orientation', 'respect for hierarchy and authority' and 'talent management'. Machiavelli's philosophy has also been applied in some social and personality studies by psychologists. Machiavellianism (often abbreviated 'Mach') has been described as a person's tendency to use manipulation over others for personal gain. In the 1960's, Richard Christie and Florence L. Geis developed a test for measuring a person's level of Machiavellianism (Wikipedia) as follows:

High Machiavellianism (**high Mach**): Scoring 60 and above (out of 100)
Low Machiavellianism (**low Mach**): Scoring below 60 (out of 100)

A person with high Mach can be described as pragmatic, realistic, no-nonsense and thus maintains emotional distance when interacting with others. To a high Mach person, the results/goals justify the means. Thus, he or she will never reveal his real motives to others unless necessary. The high Mach personality works well and will be productive when directly interacting with others, particularly when the situation has few rules and regulations. A person with low Mach does not believe in manipulating others in order to achieve his or her goal. Thus, the low Mach personality subscribes to leading a clean, moral life.

POLITICAL IDEOLOGIES AND POLITICAL SYSTEMS

In contemporary times, the world can be categorized into two types of political systems based on the political ideologies or roots of Individualism and Collectivism.

Individualism: It refers to the philosophy that an individual should have freedom in his economic and political pursuits. Individualism stresses that the interests of the individual should take precedence over the interests of the state. The intellectual root of individualism is based on the premise that the welfare of society is best served by letting people pursue their own economic self-interest. Besides this, individualism emphasizes on the importance of guaranteeing individual freedom, self-expression and political choice or rights.

Collectivism: It refers to a philosophy whereby the needs of society as a whole are generally viewed as being more important than individual freedom. The intellectual root of collectivism is based on the premise that the basic means of production, distribution and exchange should be owned by the state. Besides this, collectivists believe that if individual freedom is not restricted, a few successful capitalists will benefit at the expense of the workers.

The political system of a country determines who makes the decisions of governance and how those decisions are made. Political systems can be categorized into two inter-related dimensions:

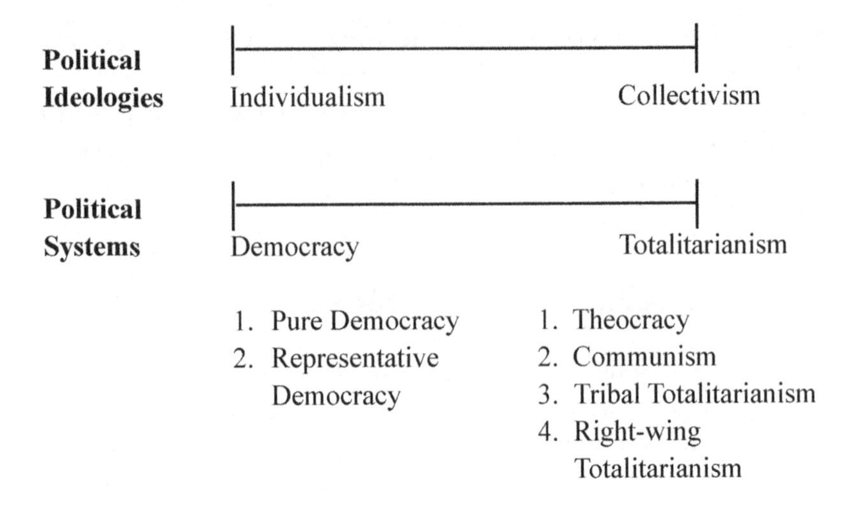

Political System: Democracy

1. Pure Democracy

Pure democracy was only practiced in ancient Greece where the citizens were directly involved in the governing of a country.

2. Representative Democracy

In today's contemporary societies, representative democracy is practiced where citizens periodically elect individuals to represent them in the governing of a country. These elected representatives then form a government, whose function is to make decisions on behalf of the electorate. If the representative democracy fails to perform this job adequately, they can be voted down at the next election. Some of the key tenets of democracy include the individual right to freedom of expression, opinion and organization, a free media, regular elections with limited terms for elected representatives, universal adult suffrage, a fair court system, a non-political police force and armed services, and relatively free access to state information. Many Western and Eastern countries practice representative democracy such as the United States, England, Japan, South Korea, Singapore, Malaysia, Thailand, Indonesia and many others.

Political system: Totalitarianism

1. Theocracy

   This is when political power is monopolized by a party that governs according to religious principles. Some of the countries in the Middle East and the African continent practice theocratic totalitarianism.

2. Communism

   2.1 Socialism advocates that everything in the country belongs to the State.

   2.2 Communist socialism believes that socialism can only be achieved through violent revolution and a totalitarian dictatorship.

3. Tribal Totalitarianism

   This occurs when a political party that represents the interests of a particular tribe monopolizes power. Some African countries still continue with such practices.

4. Right-wing Totalitarianism

   Permits individual economic freedom but restricts individual political freedom.

DEVELOPING A GRACIOUS SOCIETY

In contemporary times, Singapore is an example of a Confucian society with soft legalism. For the past four decades, Singapore has established an effective education system reinforced by Confucian values and ethics, as one of its "soft" infrastructures. In addition, Singapore has an established legal structure and system with good reinforcement. Today, Singapore enjoys a good social order (low social unrest and low industrial strikes) with one of the lowest crime rates and lowest corruption rates in many world surveys. How has Singapore done it?

Over the past few decades, the Singapore government has subscribed to Confucian teachings. According to Confucius (in the Analects: 4,13), in governing a country, one must circumscribe the people with ritual, and allow and accept the opinions of others. When a country is orderly, knowledgeable persons will emerge, but when a country is disorderly, only foolish persons will speak up (the Analects: 5,20). Confucius emphasized that a country and society should be governed by an upright government. It is only when the government is upright that people can be made upright. In his Analects (13,13), the Master said, *"If a person can be personally upright, what difficulty is there in government? But if a person cannot be personally upright, how can others be made upright?"* (Waley, 1999). When Xian asked about shame, the Master said (in the Analects: 14,1), *"When the State is orderly, (becoming an official and) receiving a salary is honorable; but when the State is disorderly, to (remain an official and) receive a salary is shameful."* (Khu *et al.*, 1991). Being an upright and non-corrupt government are essential qualities of a good government. This is one of the Confucian ethics that the Singapore government had strongly adhered to.

Although Xunzi subscribed to the idea that man's nature is evil, he believed that ritual and moral principles could make people moral. In addition, he also emphasized the importance of establishing a proper legal system with a penal code. On the one hand, it is important to continuously emphasize the Confucian values of moral ethics and responsibility. On the other hand, the reinforcement of the laws cannot be ignored. In Singapore, on the one hand, the emphasis of civil-mindedness is embedded in the school curriculum. On the other hand, they also implement strict laws with harsh punishments for those who break the laws in Singapore, regardless of citizenship.

For example, in order to discourage littering, besides education, the Singapore government uses the 'corrective work order' in addition to fines to deter or punish litter bugs, especially repeat offenders. For those caught littering, especially in repeat offence cases, they are required to sweep the streets in public as punishment, besides paying fines. Another example relates to vandalism in Singapore. In 2010, two foreigners were caught vandalizing the 'mass transit train' (MRT) and one of them was convicted and received a jail term and caning. Although the laws are strict and the punishments are harsh in Singapore, the incidents of crime or other form of social disorder are still recorded among the lowest.

The Singapore government continuously strives to make the nation one of the best cities to live in the world by creating a gracious society with good social security and social order.

The New Global Rule

In the early 20th century, there was a 'battle of ideas' with regards to the ideal type of economic system and the role of government in an economy:

(a) Centrally-planned/ Controlled Economy versus Free Market Economy

In a centrally-planned economy, every aspect of the economy such as 'what to produce?', 'how to produce?' and 'for whom to produce?' is solely decided by the central government. Every aspect of the economy is planned and controlled by the central government. In the 1920's, the Soviet Union was formed to practice the centrally-planned economic concept followed by China in 1949. Many other countries in the world such as Vietnam in Southeast Asia, North Korea in Northeast Asia and Cuba in Central America practiced a similar centrally-planned economy.

In contrast, the free market economy evolved from the political ideology and system of individualism and democracy which believes that the economy should be driven by the private sector instead of the public sector. In a free market economy, also known as capitalism, it is the private sector who determines 'what to produce?', 'how to produce?' and 'for whom to produce?' to address the market forces of demand and supply. Through the interaction of demand and supply, an equilibrium price serves as a 'traffic light', telling the market to produce more or less of a particular good or service. From the utilitarian approach (by Mozi), every individual interest will be best served in a market economy. From the modern economic perspective, the market economy will best serve individual interests based on Xunzi's assumption that 'man is selfish and greedy'. If a man is selfish, he will act in a manner by which his personal interests will be best served. If a man is greedy, he will work hard to earn and accumulate wealth.

In 1979, China (the country with the largest populace in the world) had moved towards economic reform – reforming from a centrally-planned to a market economy. In 1989, the Soviet Union had resolved its issues by reforming politically and economically. In a way, that ended socialism as the way of ruling after having been in practice for 70 years.

(b) More Government Intervention versus Less Government Intervention

In the 21st century, most countries in the world are ruled by the democratic system and moving their economies towards capitalism or market economy. The questions are: What is the role of the government in the economy? What constitutes a good government? In defining the role of the government in the economy and what constitutes a good government, it can be defined in terms of:

- Governing more

  OR
- Governing less

In the early 20th century, there was a battle of ideas as to the role of the government. The Chicago School of Economics and Austrian School of Economics subscribed to the idea that the government should not interfere with the economy while the Keynesian School of Economics tried to justify government interference. To the Chicago and Austrian Schools of Economics, the interests of the economy are best taken care of by the market – "markets work, governments don't". The Keynesian School of Economics encouraged the government to regulate the economy, such as to regulate the financial market, the stock market, and even capitalism itself. The battle of ideas evolved into a battle between the economists, Lord Maryard Keynes and Hayek where Keynes tried to justify government interference in the economy while Hayek believed that the market would take care of itself with minimum government interference.

In the 21st century, with the shifting of the global economic power from the Western nations (America and Europe) to Asia (China, Japan, and the four Newly Industrialized countries of East Asia, namely Hong Kong, Singapore, South Korea and Taiwan, as well as emerging economies like Indonesia and India), the new global rule will experience these changes:

(i) From 'country-to-country' to 'region-to-region' – the formation of regional economic cooperation such as EU, NAFTA, AFTA and APEC, just to name a few, will be intensified. There will be a balance of power between the East and the West.

(ii) From competition to collaboration - competition among countries and regions will move more towards collaboration. For the world to collaborate more, a comprehensive multilateral set of **'rules of law'** has to be agreed upon and enforced. The world needs to witness more rules and regulations in respect to:

a. Banking and financial institutions by World Bank - WB (to avoid another major financial or credit crisis). Banks and other financial institutions need more comprehensive regulations, for instance, maintaining a safe deposit-capital ratio (a form of financial gearing), prudent lending guidelines and keeping a proper lending portfolio, just to name a few;

b. Currency market by International Monetary Fund - IMF (to avoid another major current crisis). Unnecessary currency devaluating or revaluation by any major economy will result in a currency war. Appropriate central bank intervention to discourage unnecessary appreciation or depreciation of its own currency due to speculation is a **MUST** and not an option;

c. World trade by the World Trade Organization - WTO (emphasis should be on free trade as well as fair trade). Better and fairer treatment to developing and less-developed countries in the area of 'terms of trade' is necessary. Besides this, any form of trade imbalance among countries (either deficit or surplus) that persists into the medium or long term should be rectified;

d. Competitiveness should focus on productivity/efficiency and innovation (through science and technology such as biotech and nanotech);

e. Moving from 'fast growth' to 'balanced growth' (developmental) through: narrowing the gap between the rich and the poor, green technology/economy (less exploitation of resources and less emission of carbon) and being environmentally-friendly. For any country, sustainable economic growth and development should be done with long-term equilibrium in perspective. Any economic growth done at the expense of (or overly-dependent on) public debt, export market, too much domestic consumption, being too resource-based, or not environmentally-friendly will not be sustainable; and

f. Better rules and regulations and enforcement is ensured to maintain 'order' and 'fair play' at the micro, national and global levels of the economy. At the micro or industry level, there will be a higher level of collaboration and strategic alliance to replace unhealthy competition.

At the national level, better enforcement in property rights, copyrights and patent rights should be implemented. Countries need to adopt a more open policy in terms of trade and investment with greater mobility of labor and capital among countries, at least within the region.

At the global level, economic cooperation and integration should replace destructive (lose-lose) head-on competition. In the 21st century, **'rule by law'** will need to re-emphasized and reinforced to ensure a more 'orderly, stable and harmonious' world. The role of the three global organizations that are the

World Bank (WB), World Trade Organization (WTO) and International Monetary Fund (IMF) will be more emphasized. All members of these global organizations need to closely follow and operate within the rules and regulations set by these organizations. The legal rights of these organizations and their power to 'punish' non-compliance by their members needs to be strengthened.

The best way to sustain world order and maintain universal harmony is to 'curb man's greed and selfishness' – based on the definition of man as evil by Xunzi. Many of mankind's problems today are due to their selfishness in exploiting natural resources to satisfy personal acquired desires and greed. In Book 7 of Xunzi that discussed the 'Discourse of Nature', he wrote that a good government will always respond to the constancy of Nature's course and thus, good fortune will follow. To Xunzi, if a person ignores the basic undertakings and spends extravagantly, then Nature cannot enrich us. In the long run, Nature will not bring good fortune. If one does not conform to the Way (the principles of Nature), catastrophes and calamities will be of a different order – famine, sickness and inauspicious or freak events will cause misfortune (Knoblock, 1999).

Leading a simple life – with simple food, clothing and shelter – does not require a lot of money. As long as one knows when to be contented, everybody can lead a simple and carefree life like the masters, Lao Zi and Zhuang Zi.

The world needs to learn to live with less and thus, reduce the pressure of forever increasing aggregate demand. This is the best and only way to reduce or even curb the inflationary pressure of the world economy especially cost-push inflation. In this manner, it can avoid another 'oil crisis' or 'energy crisis' or even 'resource crisis' – the worst kind of economic disease – caused by supply shock – stagflation (high inflation coupled with high unemployment)!

CHAPTER 5 THE BUREAUCRATIC ORGANIZATION

EVOLUTION OF MANAGEMENT – THE BUREAUCRATIC ORGANIZATION

The **bureaucratic organizational** approach is a sub-field of the classical perspective that looks at the organization as a whole. Max Weber (1864-1920) introduced management on an impersonal, rational basis through defined authority and responsibility, formal record-keeping, and separation of management and ownership (Daft, 2008).

Weber's idea of organization was the bureaucracy: a system that incorporated division of labour, hierarchy, rules and procedures, written decisions, promotion based on technical qualifications, and separation of ownership and management. In a bureaucratic organization, managers do not depend on personality to successfully give orders, but rather on the legitimate power invested in their managerial hierarchy or positions. Some of the key components of a bureaucratic organization are:

(1) The use of formal rules, regulations and procedures – the extensive use of guidelines in guiding, circumscribing and controlling the behaviors of all employees at work.

(2) The concept of rationality – the management uses the most efficient means or methods in achieving organizational effectiveness (achieving goals or results).

(3) The principle of specialization – in order to maximize the usage of labor, the management divides the work process into simple and specialized tasks in order to maximize efficiency or productivity.

(4) The hierarchical structure – the scalar principle is strictly adhered to where power and authority increase through each level up to the top of the hierarchy.

(5) The centralized power structure – where most decisions are made at the top.

(6) The principle of impartiality – the management is impartial to all employees and thus protects all employees from the personal whims of managers.

As organizations grow and evolve, new departments and new hierarchy levels will be added to the organizational structure. Thus, the biggest challenge is how to coordinate all the different departments and divisions in achieving organizational goals, horizontally and vertically. Coordination refers to increasing the degree of collaboration and integration across departments and divisions. It is commonly observed in contemporary times that many organizations cannot function efficiently and effectively, primarily due to poor coordination. In view of globalization, the level of coordination among different business units due to geographic distance and cultural diversity has become more difficult and challenging. One good way to promote a higher level of coordination and integration among the different business units is to design and implement effective management systems, supported by flexible structures.

Benefits of a Bureaucratic Organizational Design

The term **bureaucracy** has a negative meaning in today's organizations and is commonly associated with endless rules and red tape, with well-defined divisions of labour and work specialization. Some may argue, similar to the Theory X assumptions of Douglas McGregor, that individual employees will not perform efficiently without external incentives like rules, rewards and punishments. However, there are several benefits associated with the bureaucratic organizational design. **Bureaucratic structure** involves monitoring and influencing employee behavior through rules and regulations, a code of conduct, policies and procedures, a hierarchy of authority, written documentation, and reward and punishment systems. The bureaucratic organizational design defines rules, policies and procedures explicitly for employees to follow. In this manner, it will ensure consistency and standardization in implementation that will conform to standards of measurement such as ISO requirements. Bureaucratic structure can enhance **organizational efficiency and effectiveness** in an organization, especially in terms of coordination within large-scale organizations.

Weaknesses of a Bureaucratic Organizational Design

One of the key weaknesses of bureaucratic management is slowness in decision-making. As most of the decision making is centralized at the top, decisions tend to be slow and may not truly take the local conditions into consideration. There is also a tendency for top managers to abuse their powers for personal gain. Once rigid rules and 'red tape' are installed, change tends to be slow and employees tend to follow the rules blindly or prefer the status quo. Thus, the employees refrain from using their creativity and initiative in getting things done.

DEFINING MANAGEMENT AND ORGANIZATION

The key responsibility of a manager is to coordinate resources in an effective and efficient manner to accomplish the organization's goals.

- Organizational **effectiveness** is the degree to which the organization achieves a stated goal, or succeeds in accomplishing what it tries to do.
- Organizational **efficiency** refers to the amount of resources used to achieve an organizational goal. It is based on how much raw

materials, money, and people are necessary for producing a given volume of output.

$$\text{Productivity or Efficiency} = \frac{\text{Output}}{\text{Input}}$$

The ultimate responsibility of managers is to ensure that the organization achieves **high levels of performance or results** (be effective), which is the organization's ability to attain its stated goals by using the **least amount of resources** (be efficient). A manager needs to be both efficient and effective.

Different Views of an Organization

There are five different viewpoints in defining an organization, given as follows:

1. **Employee's View**: A place to work, earn a living, as well as build a career.
2. **Manager's View**: A hierarchy with functional activities.
3. **Engineer's View**: Input ----> Process ----> Output (like a machine)
4. **System's View**: An equilibrium or balancing of different systems, sub-systems and processes with detailed procedures.
5. **Culturist's View**: A set of cultural values, beliefs, norms, rituals, rites and customs.

An organizational leader must be able to provide a holistic view of the organization by integrating the above five viewpoints (like the story of the five blind men touching the elephant). In a bureaucratic organization, the management embraces the viewpoints of the managers and engineers as the management philosophy.

Organizing is the deployment of organizational resources to achieve strategic goals. It is important for organizations to follow an organizational strategy. Strategy defines '*what* to do', while organizing defines '*how* to do it'. The organizing process leads to the creation of an organization structure, which defines how tasks are divided, resources are deployed and departments are coordinated (Daft, 2008). Organizing involves determining what tasks need to be done, who should do it, who should make the decisions, who to report to, and how much leeway there is for the person who does the work.

> Every land animal more than 15 cm high has a skeleton. This also applies to an organization. After reaching a certain size, every organization needs a formal organization structure. However, having a skeleton is insufficient for survival, as an animal requires a comprehensive and self-regulating nervous system. In an organization, besides having a formal structure, properly-defined lines of authority and responsibility, reporting relationships and lines of communication are necessary.

The following is a typical organization structure (depicted in the form of a chart) of a functional structure i.e., Production/Operation function, Marketing function and Finance & HRM function. The **organization chart** is the visual representation of an organization's structure that portrays the characteristics of a vertical structure with a number of hierarchical levels, as shown in Diagram 5.1:

Diagram 5.1
Organization Structure/Chart

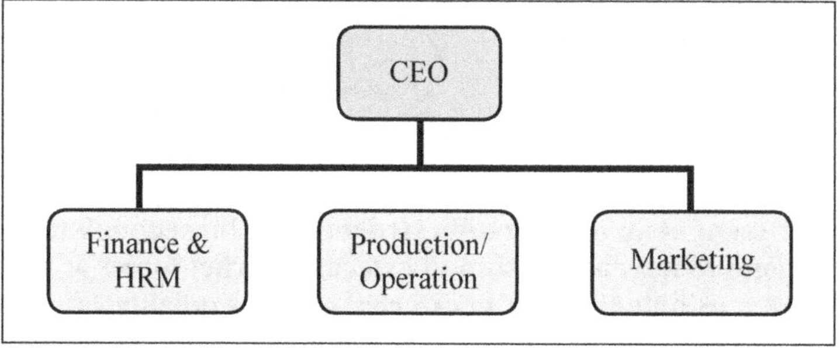

The organization structure refers to:

- Formal tasks assigned to individuals, sections, divisions and departments;
- Formal reporting relationships including lines of authority and responsibility, the number of hierarchical levels (from the highest level to the lowest level) and the span of control (which determines whether the structure is tall or short/flat); and
- Design of systems for coordination (horizontal and vertical) across different departments, divisions and sections.

ORGANIZATIONAL DESIGN

In designing an organization, several elements of the organization need to be included, such as level of work specialization, type of departmentalization, span of control, level of communication, level of formalization, centralization versus decentralization and the overall reporting relationship as per Diagram 5.2 below:

Diagram 5.2: Organizational Design

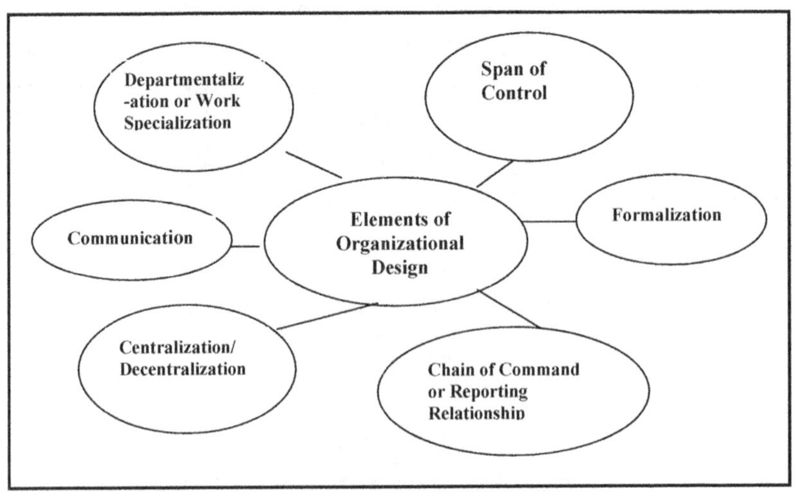

Design of an organization structure flexible enough to respond to internal needs and external market forces as well as able to adapt to external changes quickly.

Mechanistic versus Humanistic Organizational Designs

Based on the six key elements of organizational design, a company could produce and design a highly mechanistic/bureaucratic model or a highly humanistic/organic model, or a combination of both, as follows:

Mechanistic/Bureaucratic				**Humanistic/Organic**
5	4	3	2	1

Level of Practice	Level of Practice
High Work Specialization	Low Work Specialization
Centralization	Decentralization
High Formalization	Low Formalization
Narrow Span of Control (tall structure)	Wide Span of Control (flat structure)
One-way Communication	Open Communication
Rigid Reporting Relationship	Flexible Reporting Relationship

When the external business environment is stable, an organization is encouraged to use a more mechanistic system with a rigid, vertical, centralized structure and decisions made at the top. If the company's production technology uses large batches and mass production, then the company would require more standardized systems and production runs so as to ensure that production output receives high quality control and customers will receive a consistent and predictable quality.

The bureaucratic or mechanistic organizational structure and design includes the following:

(1) High Level of Work Specialization

Work specialization, sometimes called division of labor, is the degree to which organizational tasks are sub-divided into separate, yet inter-dependent jobs. In this manner, employees are required to perform small, well-defined tasks that allow a high degree of work specialization and thus, contribute to work efficiency.

However, the key disadvantage is that if an organization is overly-specialized, it will lead to employees doing only a single task day in day out, and thus bring about boredom. For example, if a job is over-specialized and thus the time to complete it is reduced from 10 minutes to 5 minutes per job cycle, then the employee will need to repeat the same process 84 times per day (based on 7 hours/420 minutes of work per day). This will make it a boring job. In 2010, several cases of labor issues in China (such as committing suicide) were principally due to being unable to cope with a monotonous work life and social life. In some companies, the management is enlarging or enriching jobs to provide greater challenges to employees or even re-designing the jobs so that they have to be performed by a team. As the saying goes, ***"If you want your employees to do a good job, give them a good job to do."*** We cannot expect employees to work enthusiastically if the job itself is monotonous, boring and poorly-designed. The job itself is the main source of work motivation and job satisfaction.

(2) Centralized Decision-Making

Centralization or decentralization refers to the type of decisions that are made at different hierarchical levels. Centralization means that the decision authority is positioned near the top of the organization's hierarchy. Decentralization refers to the decision authority being pushed further down to the lower levels of the organization's hierarchy. In a bureaucratic or mechanistic organization, most decisions are made at the top of the organization.

Factors that influence centralization of decision-making include:

a. Greater levels of consistency in decision-making are required. This is especially essential if the capability of the people is low.
b. When a company's corporate culture lacks "trust", the chance of abusing power will be high. Thus, a centralized decision will work well.
c. In times of crisis or when a company is facing the risk of failure, authority may be centralized at the top.

(3) High Level of Formalization

Formalization refers to the degree to which job processes and sub-processes within an organization, division, department and section are standardized – that is, guided by detailed work rules and procedures. In a bureaucratic organization, a highly formalized structure will be installed whereby employees have little discretion and autonomy (freedom or leeway) in deciding how the work is to be done. This will bring about a higher level of work consistency among all employees. A high level of formalization can be particularly useful in providing standardized services. For example, in McDonald's, regardless of which outlet you are visiting, the type of questions and services provided by the frontline staff remain relatively consistent.

(4) Tall Structure

A tall organization structure can be defined as a structure having many hierarchical levels, while a short organization structure can be described as having a few hierarchical levels. An organization structure, tall or short, largely depends on:

(a) The size of the company, which depends on the size of the employee base. The higher the number of employees, the taller the structure will naturally be.

(b) The span of management control is the number of employees reporting to a supervisor. For example, if a company employs 120 employees, with a span of management control of 3 (or narrow), the company will have 5 hierarchical levels. However, if the span of management control increases to 5 (or wide), the company's hierarchical level will reduce from 5 to 4 levels.

In a bureaucratic organization, the span of management control is rather narrow, thus the number of hierarchical levels will be higher or taller. This is particular useful when the employees' work is less standardized (less guided by rules and procedures), less routine, and the work location is dispersed.

(5) <u>One-Way Communication</u>

The organization structure reflects the line of command and line of authority. The line of authority is the formal and legitimate right of a manager to make decisions, give commands, as well as allocate resources and delegate work towards achieving organizational effectiveness. In a bureaucratic organization, everybody respects the line of authority and hierarchy. Not only is that authority vested in the organization position, but it is fully accepted by the subordinates. In addition, authority flows from the top level to the lower level and so does communication. Communication tends to be top-down and one-way.

(6) <u>Rigid Reporting Relationship</u>

In an organization, the chain of command is an unbroken line of authority that links all persons in an organization and shows who reports to whom (the reporting relationship).

There are two principles that need to be strictly adhered to in a bureaucratic organization, that are:

(a) Unity of Command, which means that each employee only reports and is accountable to one supervisor. If an employee has to report to two or more supervisors for his or her work, then it will violate the principle of 'Unity of Command' and this should be avoided.

(b) The scalar principle refers to a clearly defined line of authority in the organization structure that links all employees. Nobody should be left out from the line of authority no matter how ambiguous his or her position might be.

The above six (6) elements of a highly mechanistic organization structure is put forward by the bureaucracy model. If an organization grows from small to medium size or even enters the door to becoming large size, it is inevitable that the organization moves from an organic to mechanistic organizational design. Although a mechanistic organizational design could enhance organizational efficiency in achieving goals, it has to be flexible to the external environment at the same time in order to survive and excel.

BUREAUCRATIC CONTROL

In a bureaucratic organization, installing control mechanisms is the key process through which managers regulate organizational activities such as quality control to improve production quality, customer service, office productivity as well as elimination of bottlenecks. Organizations rely on quality control inspectors and supervisors to complement the equipment in ensuring high quality service and products. In this manner, organizational efficiency and effectiveness will be enhanced.

In monitoring and influencing employee behavior, the organization uses rules, policies, a hierarchy of authority and a reward and punishment system. Bureaucratic control relies on the formal hierarchy of authority and close personal supervision. In contemporary times, some organizations require all employees to read and sign a formal document called a "Code of Ethics" in controlling their behavior while executing their duties. A code of ethics is a formal statement of an organization's moral values and principles concerning ethics and social issues. It communicates to employees what the company stands for. The Code of Ethics could include some of the following:

- Comply with safety, health, and security regulations.
- Demonstrate courtesy, respect, honesty and fairness.
- Illegal drugs and alcohol at work are prohibited.
- Manage personal finances well.
- Exhibit good attendance and punctuality.
- Follow directives of supervisors.
- Do not use abusive language.
- Dress in business attire.
- Firearms at work are prohibited.
- Conduct business in compliance with all laws.
- Payments for unlawful purposes are prohibited.
- Bribes are prohibited.
- Avoid outside activities that impair duties.
- Maintain confidentiality of records.
- Comply with all anti-trust and trade regulations.
- Comply with all accounting rules and controls.
- Do not use company property for personal benefit.
- Employees are personally accountable for company funds.
- Do not propagate false or misleading information.
- Make decisions without regard for personal gain.
- Convey true claims in product advertisements.
- Perform assigned duties to the best of your ability.
- Provide products and services of the highest quality.

Source: "Management" by Stephen P. Robins and Mary Coulter, Pearson Education International, 9th edition, 2007, page 166.

For multinational corporations, the Code of Ethical Conduct should ideally embrace the following key categories:

(a) Respect for Basic Human Rights

- Respect fundamental human rights of freedom of speech, rights of life, rights of privacy and others.
- Do not discriminate against race, religion, language, gender, ethnic origin or political affiliation.

(b) Protect the Environment

- Follow local environmental protection laws.
- Be actively involved in local environmental protection against any negative externalities such as air pollution, water pollution and noise pollution.
- Help in repairing any damage to the environment and adopt green technology in conducting the business.
- Refrain from over-exploitation of local natural resources.
- Conform to local economic and development policies.

(c) Employment Practices

- Follow local employment laws and practices.
- Increase local employment opportunities and improve labor practices.
- Promote equal employment opportunities to the local people.
- Respect local unions and bargaining rights.

(d) Technology Transfer

- Be actively involved in research and development activities.
- Engage local people in technology transfer.

In implementing the "Code of Ethics", an organization could:

- Form an ethics committee (comprises of executives from different departments) to oversee the organization's ethics by ruling on questionable issues and discipline violations.
- Appoint a chief ethics officer - a company executive who oversees all aspects of ethics and legal compliance.
- Provide ethics orientation and training programs to exiting employees and new employees to help them deal with ethical issues and translate the values stated in the code of ethics into day-to-day behavior.

In today's new workplace, many organizations are moving toward increased control, especially in terms of corporate governance. **Corporate governance** is a system of governing an organization whereby the interests of all shareholders are protected. In this respect, the roles and responsibilities of the Board of Directors have to be properly spelt out and audited. In respect to financial reporting, the balance sheet and profit/loss statement has to be scrutinized.

In today's fast-moving environment, under-control can be a problem for many corporate leaders, leading to issues such as corporate scandals and unethical behavior. Many organizations resort to monitoring employees' emails and internet usage to ensure their efforts are directed towards work outcomes. However, over-control on the part of the managers has often resulted in employees' resentment about limits on their personal freedom. Excessive control with a low-trust climate could lead to demoralization and thus, lack of motivation to work. Lack of control or oversight, however, has caused some companies to suffer financial losses, in some cases, at the expense of the companies' reputation and credibility. Besides adopting the right corporate values to circumscribe the employees' ethical behavior, it is essential for all organizations to adopt:

a. explicit rules and policies;
b. high legal and professional standards;

c. 'check and balance' control management and operating systems;
d. effective employee procurement and selection system;
e. an effective appraisal and reward system with a strong emphasis on character; and
f. strong and effective leadership.

MANAGEMENT AND OPERATING SYSTEM

Efficiency and effective organizations need an effective management and operating system to support their day-to-day management. In fact, installing an effective management and operating system will not just make poor management better but can definitely make average management good. Installing an effective management and operating system is part and parcel of a control mechanism and a bureaucratic organization. A comprehensive system not only prevents defiant behavior, but also encourages good and positive behavior. In contemporary management studies, systems theory defines the organization as an open system that constantly interacts with the external environment in order to survive or even excel.

An engineer sees an organization like a system with input-process-output. This is in line with the system viewpoint where all organizations operate in an open-system that is constantly interacting with the environment. Internally, the organization is like a separate entity or a system with a sub-system. Each sub-system is further divided into processes and sub-processes, where each sub-process can be defined in terms of activities. The organizational process covers the current ways of getting things done and also covers the whole theory and definition of a business. The assumptions on which organizations and their processes have been built since one to two decades ago will soon no longer fit in the "Information/Digital Age". We are gradually moving away from the "Industrial Age" which started 300-400 years ago. They way we view the external environment such as the economic structure, the industry and market structures, the customers and the technology are all different from how they were two to three decades ago. Business or Organizational Process Reengineering is a technique to radically improve profit performance and create sustainable competitive advantage by challenging and redesigning the core business and its processes using operational, technical and business knowledge in a collective way. A simple System Analysis Framework as per Figure 5.1 is proposed as follows:

Figure 5.1
System Analysis Framework

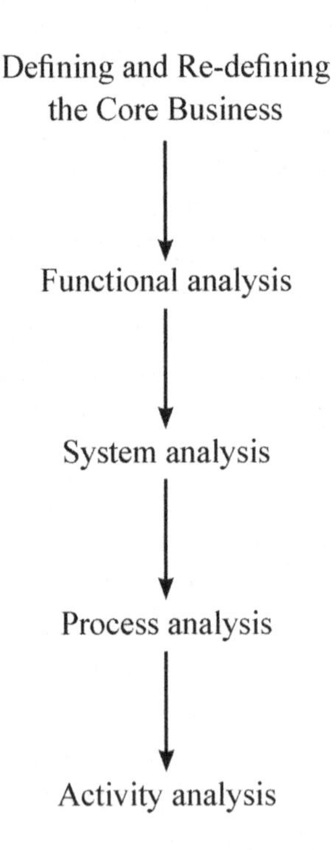

The overall function of an organization can be divided into several different functions such as the Production/Operation Department, Marketing Department, Finance and Accounting Department and Human Resource Department, just to name a few. Each functional department is supported by several different functions. For example, the Human Resource Department could design and implement a comprehensive "Performance Management System" (PMS) to manage the overall performance of its people. The PMS could then be further divided into sub-systems such as the Key Performance Indicators (KPI) system, Appraisal system, Reward system and Development system. Each sub-system could then be divided into processes and sub-processes (or activities).

In conducting a proper system analysis, a model of a process/activity framework is proposed as per Diagram 5.3. Primarily, each system comprises of input, process/activity and output. The key purpose of the review is to improve in focus on increasing quality, improving services, reducing costs and reducing cycle-time so as to enhance "Customer Value" – for both internal and external customers.

Diagram 5.3

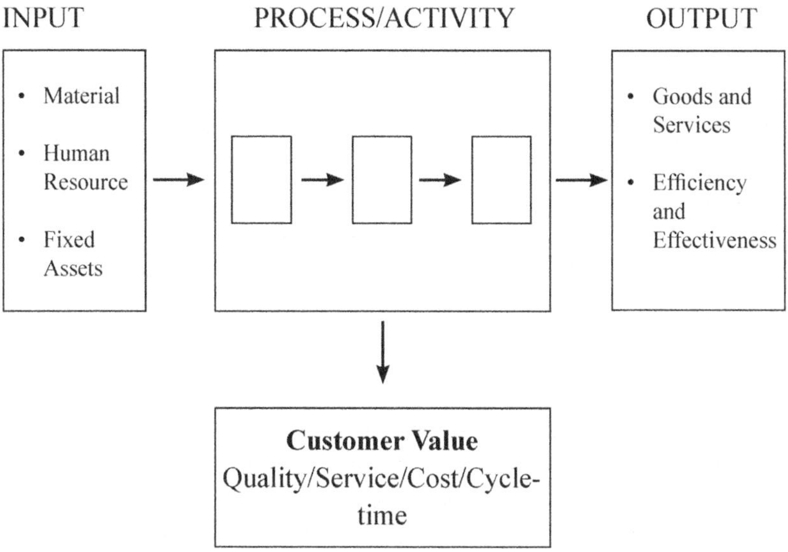

INPUT
- Material
- Human Resource
- Fixed Assets

→ PROCESS/ACTIVITY: □ → □ → □ →

OUTPUT
- Goods and Services
- Efficiency and Effectiveness

↓

Customer Value
Quality/Service/Cost/Cycle-time

Activity Analysis

For each of the processes, an activity analysis will be conducted. The steps involved are:

(a) Prepare a list of activities that are going to be performed.

(b) Prepare a definition of each activity and determine the work-load measure (time and cost study).

(c) Classify all the activities into:

- Primary and secondary activities
- Value-added and non-value-added activities

Table 5.1
Primary and Secondary Activity Analysis

	Value-added	**Non-value-added**
Primary activity	Directly contribute to your KPI – **continuous improvement.**	Indirectly contribute to your KPI- **simplify or eliminate them.**
Secondary activity	Support the primary work objectives – **simplify them.**	Indirectly support your work activities – **eliminate them where possible.**

The Role of Information Technology

In the Information or Digital Age, the role and the use of Information Technology in re-engineering the business or work processes is critical. The following Table 5.2 provides the difference the "old rule" and the "new rule" about Information Technology and its impacts on today's organizational practice.

Table 5.2
The Role of Information Technology

Old Rule	New Rule
Information can appear in only one place at one time.	Information can appear simultaneously in as many places as it is needed.
Only experts can perform complex work.	A generalist can do the work of an expert.
Business must choose between centralization and decentralization.	Businesses can simultaneously reap the benefits of centralization and decentralization.
Managers make all decisions.	Decision-making is part of everyone's job.
Field personnel need offices where they can receive, store, retrieve, and transmit information.	Field personnel can send and receive information wherever they are.
The best contact with a potential buyer is personal contact.	The best contact with a potential buyer is effective contact.
You have to find out where things are.	Things tell you where they are.
Plans get revised periodically.	Plans get revised instantaneously.

Adopted from "Reengineering the Corporation: A Manifesto for Business Revolution" by Hammer ,Michael and Champy, James, 1994.

"Breakpoint priorities" should be market-driven or result-driven. The key focus for reengineering or breakpoint is as follows:

- Time (cycle or lead)/Speed (faster)
- Quality (better)
- Cost (cheaper)
- Reliability
- Process Design
- Flexibility
- Differentiation

These are some of the key break-points that can bring about improved organizational efficiency and effectiveness. Always find new ways to keep the costs low by increasing productivity (or efficiency). Find new and better ways of getting things done by studying the work processes and sub-processes. Set a goal to increase overall productivity says 5%-10% per year. Monitor your expenses (overheads) closely and ensure that your expenses increase slower than your revenues increase. Set **Key Performance Indicators** (KPIs) or Productivity Ratios that are applicable to all different functional departments in the organization are presented in Table 5.3.

Table 5.3
Key Performance Indicators/Productivity Ratios

Department	Key Performance Indicators/ Productivity Ratios
Production or Operation	■ Production output per net machinery/equipment ■ Machine downtime ■ Reject rate due to technical problem ■ Reject rate due to human error ■ Rework rate due to technical problem ■ Rework rate due to human error ■ Recovery rate from raw material ■ Production output per factory built-up area ■ Number of occupational accident
Marketing	■ Gross profit margin ■ Sales per sales-person ■ Sales growth ■ Market share growth ■ Number of complaints received ■ Percentage of repeated sales versus new sales ■ Back orders ■ Return of goods by customer ■ Response time to enquiry ■ Delivery time
Finance and Accounting	■ Accuracy of financial statement ■ Timeliness of financial statement ■ Average cost of financing ■ Return on Assets ■ Return on Investment

Department	Key Performance Indicators/ Productivity Ratios
Human Resource Development	■ Direct labour turnover ■ Indirect labour turnover ■ Direct labour absenteeism rate ■ Number of industrial relation case ■ Number of grievances filed ■ Number of warning (oral or written) issued
Information Technology	■ Number of system down-time ■ Average time of system up-time ■ Confidential leaks

Manage the data. Everything you do, you must be able to measure them. In that way, you can track the result and measure the effectiveness. For example, if you spend $1 million on advertisement, you need to measure the impact on sales before and after the advertisement. Learn to test and measure everything.

Embrace learning into your business. You must understand that:

Learning = Earning

Learning always comes before earning. At time, you need to engage an outsider or external party to do the 'check and balance' – you simply needs another set of eyes to see and check how your business is going.

Total Quality Management (TQM) System

TQM system focuses on infusing quality into every process and activity in a company. The TQM philosophy and system focus on teamwork and internal, increasing customer satisfaction, and efficiency (in terms of lowering costs). Organizations implement TQM by encouraging managers and employees to collaborate across functions and departments (from marketing and production to finance and HRM functional departments), as well as with other stakeholders such as customers and suppliers, to identify areas for improvement. Some of the following TQM concept and system that are relevant in today's organizational practices:

(a) International Quality Standards (ISOs)

ISO certification is based on a set of international standards for quality management systems established by the International Standards Organization in Geneva, Switzerland. Nowadays, many organizations work toward the certification of ISO especially when penetrating and exporting to European countries.

(b) Benchmarking

Benchmarking is the process of measuring products, services, and practices and then compared (or "benchmark against") with the best company in the industry or those companies recognised as industry leaders. A company would carefully selects the right competitor(s) worthy of benchmarking and then emulating their processes and procedures.

(c) Balanced Score Card

Balanced score card focuses on four key elements that include business process, customer service, financial performance and potential growth. Organizations that implement balanced score card focus on target setting, evaluation of performance and action plans.

There are many other organizational efficiency and effectiveness systems or tools available in the market such as Six Sigma, Business Process Reengineering (BPR), Kaizen Management, Just-in-Time (JIT) Inventory Management and Zero Defect Management.

In a bureaucratic organization, all systems, processes and activities (human and mechanical) must be **Measured, Monitored and Managed** (the **3 Ms approach**). Nothing should be left to chance. Thus, the bureaucratic organization focuses on:

- 'Management By System' instead of 'Management By Wandering Around'
- 'Management By Rules/Regulations' instead of 'Management By Relationship'

In today's organizational control, managers need to design systematic process through which managers regulate organizational activities to make them consistent with the expectations established in plans with objectives and standards of performance. To effectively control an organization, managers require information that is timely, accurate and reliable to ensure steps can be taken to correct (if there is any deviations) or even to prevent deviations before they occur.

**"If you want one year of prosperity, motivates people.
If you want ten years of prosperity, builds structure and system.
If you want one hundred years of prosperity, develops a corporate culture."**

CONCLUSION

In reviewing Chinese history, philosophy, culture and tradition, I have often asked, "What are the key differences and similarities between Chinese and Western culture?" Based on my brief study and review of Confucianism, Daoism, Utilitarianism and Legalism which evolved during the Warring States and Spring and Autumn Periods, some of the key differences and similarities between the Chinese and Western culture and philosophy of life can be simplified as per Diagram 1 below:

Diagram 1: The Ultimate Goals of Life

Chinese Culture and Philosophy of Life

1st School of Thought
- Ethics and morality values
- Humanism and relationships
- Strict in soft rules and regulations
- Frugality in the usage of resources

2nd School of Thought
- Seeks contentment and leads a simple life
- Satisfy without understanding and knowing
- Preserve Nature and the Environment

Western Culture and Philosophy of Life

1st School of Thought
- Spiritualism through religion

2nd School of Thought
- Materialism and the creation of wealth
- Science and Technology
- Invention and innovation
- Better techniques and methods for the betterment of life

→

Ultimate Goals
- In search of happiness.
- In search of the meaning of life.
- To uncover the secrets of Nature or the Universe.

In examining the evolution of Chinese culture and philosophy of life in the past 2,000 to 3,000 years, there are certain strengths and weaknesses revealed of the different schools of thought. However, it is quite meaningless to glorify the strengths and criticize the weaknesses of the past. A good and living culture is a culture that is subject to change by constantly interacting with the environments. The Chinese culture needs to continue to examine its own heritage (thoughts and systems), preserve what is good and relevant to contemporary times and discard what is bad or irrelevant to current times. At the same time, Chinese culture needs to open up and continuously interact with other cultures in the world as well as absorb whatever is worthy of another's culture. In this manner, the Chinese culture will always stay relevant.

For thousands of years, the Chinese have been known to be adaptable whereby they can be found in all corners of the world and found to be doing well. The greatest wisdom of the Chinese is **"Adaptability"**. In the 21st century, China and the Chinese, as one of the oldest civilizations, will continue to play an active role in the world, not just in the case of economic activity but culturally as well. At the time the Chinese culture has truly integrated with world culture, China can play the role of spearheading and promoting a Universal Culture of the world.

In 1988, 75 Nobel Prize winners made a statement in Paris that if humankind is to survive in the 21st century, they must draw **wisdom from Confucius**. The Chinese culture, especially neo-Confucianism that embraces Confucianism, Daoism, Buddhism and Legalism will remain as the greatest strength of China, and all Chinese, for many centuries and generations to come.

BIBLIOGRAPHY

Ames, Roger T. (1983), "The Art of Rulership", University of Hawaii Press.

Chen, Ming-Jer (2002), "Transcending Paradox: The Chinese "Middle Way"
Perspective", Asia Pacific Journal of Management, 19, pp. 179-199.

De Bary, William Theodore, Chan Wing-Tsit and Watson Bunton (1960), "The Sources
of Chinese Tradition", Columbia University Press.

Fung, Yu-Lan, "A Short History of Chinese Philosophy", The Free Press, 1948.

Heider, John (1994), "The Tao of Leadership", SSMS publishing division.

Khu, John B, Vincentra B.M. Khu, William B.S. Khu and Jose B.K. Khu (1991), "The
Confucius Bible", Granhill Corporation.

Knoblock, John (translator), "Xunzi I", Library of Chinese Classics, Hunan People's
Publishing House, Foreign Language Press, China, 1999.

Knoblock, John (translator), "Xunzi II", Library of Chinese Classics, Hunan People's
Publishing House, Foreign Language Press, China, 1999.

Lau, D.C. (1963), "Lau Tsu: Tao Te Ching", Penguin Classics.

Lau, D.C. (1970), "Mencius", Penguin Classics.

Lau, D.C. (1979), "Confucius: The Analects", Penguin Classics.

Liang, Congjie, "The Great Thoughts of China", John Wiley & Sons, Inc., 1996.

Low, C.C., "The First Emperor of China: Qin ShiHuang", Confonian Pte Ltd, 1999.

Mei, Y.P. "The Basic of Social, Ethical and Spiritual Values in Chinese Philosophy",
The Chinese Mind: Essentials of Chinese Philosophy and Culture, edited by
Charles A Moore, Honolulu, East-West Centre Press, 1994.

Moore, Charles A. (1967), "The Chinese Mind: Essentials of Chinese Philosophy and Culture".

Ren, Changhong and Wu Jingyu, "Rise and Fall of Qin Dynasty", Asiapac Books, 2000.

Roberts, J.A.G., "A Concise History of China", Harvard University Press, 1999.

Stephen P. Robins and Mary Coulter (2007), "Management", Pearson Education International,.

Tang, C Michael, "A Victor's Reflections", Prentice Hall Press, 2000.

Tsai, Chin Chong (b), "The Sayings of Han Fei Zi", Asiapac Publication, Singapore, 1991.

Watson, Button (1964), "Han Fei Tzu", Columbia University Press.

About the Author

DR SHEH SEOW WAH (佘绍华 博士)

Qualifications:

Doctor of Business Administration, Maastricht School of Management, Netherlands

Master of Philosophy, Maastricht School of Management, Netherlands

Master of Science (Management), National University of Singapore, Singapore

Master of Business Administration, University of East Asia, Macau, China

Bachelor of Business Administration (2nd Upper), National University of Malaysia

Advanced Certificate in Teaching (Higher Education), SIM Global Education

Certificate in Teaching (Higher Education), Singapore Polytechnic, Singapore

ABOUT THE AUTHOR

SHEH is a **Research Consultant** for a higher learning institution and an **Adjunct Lecturer** at the University of South Australia, supervising over 20 doctorate students in Singapore/ Hong Kong/China/Malaysia since 2002. In addition, he has been a **Management Consultant** for several years. He is also a Regional Editor of Emerald Emerging Markets Case Studies journal.

Sheh has served as a **lecturer and trainer** at several private academic institutions in Australia and Singapore for over 20 years and has taught on principles of management, organizational behavior, finance, personnel, marketing, economics, business development, cross-culture management and global business for diploma, bachelor degree and master degree programs. He was conferred a scholarship by the Public Service Department (Malaysia) to pursue his Bachelor of Business Administration (2nd upper). He was also awarded a research scholarship from the National University of Singapore to pursue his Master of Science (Management) degree. His scope of research includes Chinese values, Chinese leadership, Chinese family business and Change Management, focusing on medium- to large-sized organizations.

Made in the USA
Monee, IL
22 June 2021

71985298R00095